MOBILE LEARNING MINDSET

THE PARENT'S GUIDE TO SUPPORTING DIGITAL AGE LEARNERS

CARL HOOKER

International Society for Technology in Education
PORTLAND, OREGON • ARLINGTON, VIRGINIA

Mobile Learning Mindset
The Parent's Guide to Supporting Digital Age Learners
Carl Hooker

Editor: *Emily Reed*
Copy Editor: *Kristin Landon*
Cover Design: *Brianne Beigh*
Book Design and Production: *Kim McGovern*

Library of Congress Cataloging-in-Publication Data
Names: Hooker, Carl, author.
Title: Mobile learning mindset : the parent's guide to supporting digital age learners / Carl Hooker.
Description: Portland, Oregon : International Society for Technology in Education, [2017] | Includes bibliographical references.
Identifiers: LCCN 2017007015 (print) | LCCN 2016046976 (ebook) | ISBN 9781564843968 (pbk.) | ISBN 9781564846525 (mobi) | ISBN 9781564846532 (epub) | ISBN 9781564846549 (pdf)
Subjects: LCSH: Mobile communication systems in education. | Education—Parent participation. | Home and school.
Classification: LCC LB1044.84 .H67 2017 (ebook) | LCC LB1044.84 (print) | DDC 371.33—dc23
LC record available at https://lccn.loc.gov/2017007015

First Edition
ISBN: 978-1-56484-396-8
Ebook version available

Printed in the United States of America

ISTE® is a registered trademark of the International Society for Technology in Education.

About ISTE

The International Society for Technology in Education (ISTE) is the premier nonprofit organization serving educators and education leaders committed to empowering connected learners in a connected world. ISTE serves more than 100,000 education stakeholders throughout the world.

ISTE's innovative offerings include the ISTE Conference & Expo, one of the biggest, most comprehensive ed tech events in the world—as well as the widely adopted ISTE Standards for learning, teaching and leading in the digital age and a robust suite of professional learning resources, including webinars, online courses, consulting services for schools and districts, books, and peer-reviewed journals and publications. Visit iste.org to learn more.

Also by Carl Hooker

Mobile Learning Mindset: The District Leader's Guide to Implementation

Mobile Learning Mindset: The Principal's Guide to Implementation

Mobile Learning Mindset: The Coach's Guide to Implementation

Mobile Learning Mindset: The Teacher's Guide to Implementation

Mobile Learning Mindset: The IT Professional's Guide to Implementation

To see all books available from ISTE, please visit iste.org/resources.

About the Author

Carl Hooker has been involved in education since graduating from the University of Texas in 1998. He has been in a variety of positions in both Austin Independent School District (ISD) and Eanes ISD, from first grade teacher to virtualization coordinator.

Hooker is now director of innovation and digital learning at Eanes ISD. He is also the founder of the learning festival iPadpalooza (http://ipadpalooza.com). As director, he uses his background in both education and technology to bring a unique vision to the district and its programs. During his tenure, Eanes has jumped into social media, adopted the Google Apps for Education, and started to build a paperless environment with Google Docs. Hooker helped spearhead the Learning and Engaging through Access and Personalization (LEAP) program, which put 1:1 iPads into the hands of all K–12 students at Eanes.

Hooker has been a part of a strong educational shift toward technology integration. From his start as a teacher to his current district technology leadership role, he has always held one belief: Students need to drive their own learning. He realizes the challenges in our current public educational institutions and meets them head-on. His unique blend of educational background, technical expertise, and humor makes him a successful driving force for this change. Hooker also works as a keynote speaker and consultant through his company HookerTech, LLC.

Contents

Contents

Preface

In January 2010, Steve Jobs took the stage at a major Apple event to announce the creation of a device that was in between a laptop and a smartphone. When he announced the iPad, the reviews were mixed. Wasn't this something that had been tried before, even with Apple's MessagePad? (http://en.wikipedia.org/wiki/MessagePad) How was this going to work in mainstream society when it was bigger and bulkier than a phone and didn't have the keyboard of a laptop?

At the time of the announcement, I was a virtualization coordinator for the district. The technology director (my boss at the time) looked at me with wonder when I showed my excitement over this announcement. "This is going to change the face of education," I told him. His response: "I bet they don't sell even a million of them. It's like a crappy version of a laptop, only you can only do one thing at a time on it. It doesn't even have a USB port!"

In retrospect, I should have taken that bet, as Apple went on to sell a million in pre-orders alone. Flash forward a few more months. On April 2nd I was promoted to the role of Director of Instructional Technology. The very next day the first-generation iPad began to be sold in U.S. stores. I point this all out to show that even with all the prep work and sweat necessary for a successful device deployment, some synergy is also required.

As Director of Instructional Technology, I was taking over a dying role of sorts. Many districts were cutting the position at that time in Texas, and some felt it was a "nice to have" more than "a need to have" position. Knowing that going in, I made it one of my personal missions to erase the thought from the minds of the purse-string holders that my position could ever become obsolete. In fact, I set out to do the exact opposite: make them think they couldn't function successfully without it.

A big part of any leadership position is assessing risks. With the announcement of the iPad, my mind immediately went to education. How could these devices help students personalize their own learning? How would they enhance engagement and the learning experience of students? Are those gains in engagement and personalization enough to justify giving every student one of these devices?

These questions and many others went through my mind and those of many of the leaders in my district in the months that followed. Ultimately, in the fall of 2010, our district took the first steps toward providing 1:1 mobile devices. Whereas some districts chose to make big splashes with their first deployment, our initiative started with a forward-thinking librarian (Carolyn Foote) purchasing six first-generation iPads for students and teachers to check out.

Enter the second synergistic event. A group of leaders including myself made a trip to Cupertino, California, for an executive briefing on Apple's ideas for iPads in education. Before lunch of the first day, the Westlake High School principal leaned over and said to us, "We need one of these for every student." At that time, iPads were considered purely consumptive devices—a nice way to read a book or take notes, but nothing in the way of creativity. That trip to Apple's headquarters changed all of that for those in the room, even those who had been skeptical.

When we returned, we went on to expand the pilot to around 70 different users. From special education students to principals to high school AP teachers, we had as many key stakeholders as possible get their hands on this device to put it through its paces. At this point the iPad 2 had just launched and had a lot more functionality for creativity than its predecessor, namely the addition of a camera.

The pilot went on to expand into Westlake High School the following fall, and eventually reached all 8,000 Eanes ISD K–12 students by the spring of 2013. Here's an early blog post right after launch of the pilot on the EanesWifi site: http://eaneswifi.blogspot.com/2011/09/wifi-pilot-gets-started.html. Along the way, we've seen the highs and lows of having a device for every student, especially one as nimble and easy-to-use as an iPad.

The Mobile Learning Mindset series chronicles that journey from the perspective of six different components. Each component was key to making the initiative as successful as it's become, and as you'll learn, they are all intertwined with each other. This series is not specifically geared toward a 1:1 or Bring Your Own Device (BYOD) initiative. It's meant to be read as a handbook for any teacher, leader, or parent who is involved with a school that is using mobile device technology in the classroom.

The first book goes into detail about what district leadership can and should do to make a mobile device initiative successful. Having a strong, clearly defined goal and vision for a district that's well-communicated is an important part of the process. From the superintendent to the school board to the district and campus level administrators, all need to be singing the same lyrics in the song of 1:1, or else it may fall flat.

The second book in the series is specifically focused on campus leaders and how they can support and showcase the initiative at the campus level. The book discusses the role the campus leader plays in terms of parent communication, teacher expectations, and highlighting student-led projects in the classroom.

The third book in the series focuses on diving into ideas and best practices for professional development around a 1:1. I've seen many a district, including my own, continue the previous practices of professional development of a "sit 'n' get" style of learning, all the while preaching about how the students need to be the center of the learning. This book focuses on how to make that shift in your organization and ideas on how to make learning more engaging for your staff.

The fourth offers an in-depth look at how mobile devices affect the classroom and what teachers can do both right out of the box and farther down the road to sustain a successful student-led learning environment. Using mobile devices just as a substitute for a textbook is a waste of money. These devices are multimedia studios of creation, but often that use is restricted by the classroom teacher. Book 4 explores models such as SAMR and tools that a teacher can use right away to shift the way learning takes place from a traditional classroom to a mobile classroom.

One major part of a mobile learning initiative is keeping community parents educated on the ins and outs of having mobile devices around the home, which is the focus of this, the fifth book, for parents. Part of the disruptive effect that mobile devices have on learning also affects the home. Parents are now facing dilemmas of social media, cyberbullying, and digital footprints that their parents never had to deal with. This book serves as an instruction manual of sorts for parents raising kids in the digital age.

Last, none of this is possible without proper technical support. From infrastructure to break-fix scenarios, having a technology services department on board is vital. The final book in the series is centered around that support. Technology changes so frequently that it is nearly impossible to create a book that has all the latest trends and gadgets. This book focuses on some necessary components of supporting a 1:1 mobile device initiative, as well as how to work with leaders, teachers, trainers, and parents on making the initiative a success.

Each book has a similar structure. Included among the chapters is one on "top 10 things not to do," an interview with an area expert in that book's particular focus, and chapters dedicated to ideas and strategies for interacting with all the other "players" in a mobile device initiative. In other words, how does a district leader support his/her teachers in this new environment? What expectations should the campus administrator have for his/her staff in terms of professional development? And conversely, how can professional development support those expectations?

All six of these components are parts of the very complex, constantly evolving machine that is a mobile learning initiative. Each plays its part, and each requires different amounts of attention and support from the other parts in order to work efficiently. Neglecting one of these components will result in the other parts having to work harder and could ultimately cause the machine to break down. My hope is that if you use this book series to learn how all the parts work, your own mobile learning machine will be a thing of beauty for your students. After all, their learning and their future is the ultimate reason to do something as bold as an initiative using mobile devices in the classroom.

Good luck, and thank you for being a part of this mobile learning revolution!

—Carl Hooker

INTRODUCTION

"Back in my day. …"

As a child raised in the mid-'80s, I regularly heard this phrase from my own parents. It often followed descriptions of some major shortcoming or their lack, as kids, of some resource that we kids took for granted. Things like, "Back in my day, we didn't have cordless phones. In fact, we had rotary dial phones, and if you had a number with a lot of 8's or 9's in it, people rarely called you."

Another favorite was, "It used to cost us 25 cents to go to the movies, which was like a week's salary back in my day."

I look back and laugh at these statements, but as I'm raising my own kids in the 21st century, as well as teaching and working with those in my district, I'm hearing this same "back in my day" phrase uttered by friends, parents, and colleagues more and more. It's almost as though the pace of change with technology has created this sizeable gap in knowledge between children of the digital age and their parents. I know the term "digital native" is bandied about a lot in educational circles, but I can tell you that it's largely a myth or excuse used by adults who simply can't fathom what kids these days are up to.

When we first started down the road of our L.E.A.P. initiative (then called the "Westlake Initiative for Innovation" or WIFI Project), one of the areas of greatest concern came from the parent community. Placing school-issued devices in the hands of kids was much more divisive in some ways than just allowing kids to bring their own devices (BYOD). Although both can be disruptive events, in the case of students bringing their own devices, the disruption is more prevalent in the classroom than in the home. When there is a school-issued mobile device initiative, the disruption is more evenly distributed between classroom and home. In some cases, parents may have opted to not allow their children to have a mobile device, but that's usurped by the school issuing one for learning.

Whether or not you as a parent agree or disagree with the decision of a school district to provide or allow devices, one thing is for certain: Mobile devices are here to stay. As Linda Rawlings, then principal of our initial 1:1 iPad pilot at Westlake High School, once told me, "That genie is already out of the bottle and there's *no* way we're putting it back in." I think, as parents, we can either reject or accept the idea that mobile devices can be a positive experience for our students' learning. If you reject this idea completely, then this might be the last paragraph you read in this book. However, if you have some curiosity or inkling of possibility toward the concept of mobile learning, I invite you to read further so that you can gain some tools and perspective on what a mobile learning initiative might mean for your own child.

How to Use This Book

This book is broken down into various chapters that will serve as both a guide and a resource for parents, depending on the state of the mobile learning initiative at your child's school. The structure of the chapters in this book mirrors the structure of the other books in the series, though the content is different. Although the intended audience is parents of students in a mobile device initiative, teachers and administrators can also gain some insights throughout on how to support the school community during this process. I've often said it "takes an iVillage" to raise a digital child, and that's certainly been the case throughout the years of our initiative.

The first four books really tackle both the "why" and "how" of mobile learning. Getting leadership on board with encouraging a learning culture and having professional learning that supports the teacher is key. This book is all about the parents supporting a mobile learning initiative at home as well as in the classroom. In the first chapter, we really focus some time and energy on understanding what research tells us about student learning with high-quality technology integration and what benefits come from a school pursuing a 1:1 mobile device initiative.

The second chapter is focused on the top 10 things *not* to do as a parent of a child in a mobile device initiative. Modeling and allowing your child some room to grow (and at times fail) with mobile devices are some things to not forget. This chapter really begins to outline many of the other chapters throughout the book when it comes to ideas and strategies for integrating mobile learning into your classroom.

Chapter 3 is an interview with Dr. Devorah Heitner (aka @DevorahHeitner on Twitter). Dr. Heitner is the author of several books including *Screenwise* and *Raising Digital Natives*. Devorah has years' worth of research that she describes during her interview, along with helpful tips for parents and educators alike.

The middle chapters cover various intricacies involved when your child has a mobile device, and what that means for their day-to-day interactions. Chapter 4 provides some common vocabulary as well as laying out the concept of digital wellness for ourselves and kids. Chapter 5 focuses primarily on one major aspect of digital wellness, screen time, and how that affects the brain, sleep, and learning.

In Chapter 6, I cover one of the most prevalent issues we face raising kids in this century: social media. Although part of social media is being aware of what is out there, in many cases, behaviors online can be reflective of behavior in real life. (Or "IRL," as the kids say it these days.)

Awareness of screen time, gaming addiction, and social media pitfalls is only the first step when it comes to really supporting a digital child. In Chapter 7, I give some examples of guidelines and rules I've come across over the years, both as a parent and as someone who speaks with parents on a regular basis.

Although guidelines and rules are effective ways to build and encourage responsible online behavior with our kids, there are times when we need to restrict certain aspects of what they do with technology and mobile devices specifically. Chapter 8 introduces some resources and tools to use when considering internet filters at home and restrictions to place on the device.

In the final two chapters, I tie together the other components of this book series and how they interact with parents supporting a mobile learning initiative. When classroom teachers and campus administrators communicate with parents about tools and resources, this can really stave off any negative behaviors before they get out of control. Finding resources for professional learning or having conversations with the technology department can go a long way in empowering you, as a parent, to raise students in this day and age.

"Easter Eggs"

According to Wikipedia, an Easter egg is "an inside joke, hidden message, or feature in an interactive work such as a computer program, video game or DVD menu screen." Why can't we also have these in books? In this book, I've hidden several Easter eggs that you'll have to uncover and discover. Some are buried in words, others in images. How do you reveal them? If you are reading this book in its paper form, you'll need to download the Aurasma app (www.aurasma.com/#/whats-your-aura) and find the trigger images to unlock the Easter eggs. Find and follow the "MLM Vision" channel to make it all work. Instructions can be found here: mrhook.it/eggs. Happy hunting!

CHAPTER 1

MAKING THE CASE FOR MOBILE LEARNING

If you are a parent reading this book, it's likely that your child's school district is involved in some sort of mobile device initiative. Maybe they're using mobile devices in carts in some classrooms, or issuing devices to each student in the school. Many schools now allow students to bring in their own devices (BYOD) and use the mini-computers in their pockets to help access information and knowledge. Regardless of the reason, you might be wondering, why are schools doing this? Why invite in the distraction and expense of students having mobile devices into schools? There must be a good reason for this besides "If you can't beat them, join them."

Background on 1:1 Initiatives

It turns out that mobile device and 1:1 initiatives are not as new as you might expect. In the mid-1980s, Apple introduced its "Apple Classrooms of Tomorrow" program as a way to infuse and integrate technology into schools. Although much of that research has evolved as the devices have become more mobile, the premise is that technology can help level the playing field and increase the speed with which students access information.

One of the earliest researchers in the field of technology integration was Dr. Ruben Puentedura. He began researching the effects of technology and learning in classrooms starting as far back as 1987. In 2001, the state of Maine used a surplus of funds to pay for the first-ever statewide 1:1 program. Following the work of a task force and years of research by both Puentedura and the noted scholar Seymour Papert, then-Governor Angus King realized the need to better prepare students for the modern world. So began their Maine Learning Technology Initiative (MLTI) program (maine.gov/mlti/), which continues to change and evolve today.

Although he has not done specific research on mobile devices in schools, educational theorist Sir Ken Robinson has written and spoken about the need for schools to not only reform, but transform themselves into more modern institutions. In his book *Out of Our Minds,* he details how schools have basically descended from the industrial revolution and assembly-line mentality of learning. In this factory model of education, everyone is processed based on the "date of manufacture" (the year they were born) and then placed on the conveyor belt to learn at a pre-set rate during pre-set times covering pre-set content.

The world that existed when that model was put in place no longer exists. Students are not leaving our schools and heading to the factory. They are entering a world that is mobile and instant. The workplace is no longer desks in a row and 9 to 5. It's now 24/7 and can be done from anywhere. Yet our schools still function in much the same way as those factories from the 1950s.

Technology doesn't solve all of these issues, but in some ways it provides a way to bend space and time. It provides students with equal access to the world's content. It allows for tasks that were previously not possible or conceivable. This is what Dr. Puentedura calls "Redefinition" in his SAMR Model of technology integration (mrhook.it/samr1). It also opens up possibilities for students that didn't exist before—assuming that teachers and schools use it properly and wisely.

National and Global Findings on 1:1 Initiatives

One of the largest studies recently released included more than three decades of research on technology integration by Dr. Puentedura himself. In the concluding summary, it states:

> Technology that supports instruction has a marginally but significantly higher average effect compared to technology applications that provide direct instruction. Lastly, it was found that the effect size was greater when applications of computer technology were for K–12, rather than computer applications being introduced in postsecondary classrooms (Higgins, Xiao, & Katsipataki, 2012).

This means that using technology by effectively integrating into a lesson ("supporting instruction") versus just allowing students to play a learning game ("providing direct instruction") is more meaningful and impactful for students. Indeed, in our district the most effective 1:1 classrooms use devices in a manner that enhances and amplifies learning outcomes. It's important to note here that in its beginning stages, a mobile learning initiative generally starts more at the substitutive level (devices being used for ebooks or note-taking) and somewhat as direct instruction in the lower grades (playing learning games).

However, as Dr. Puentedura's research points out, to have a larger effect on learning, the use of the devices needs to shift to more of a supportive role in learning. They can be used as tools to create solutions and outcomes in a personalized fashion. Although this isn't the expected daily use of mobile devices in schools (how often do you use your phone to creatively solve problems?), it is one of the advantages of having access to such devices. Pedagogy still guides much of the use of the device and its integration into learning.

The LEAP Initiative and Our Own Findings

When we started our mobile device initiative, it was based on a mix of the research just discussed, but also on feedback from our students after they had left the district. Although we had prepared students well for academia, they felt underprepared for managing their digital lives and the distractions that came with having mobile devices all around them in the workplace or college classroom. They could do well at paper-and-pencil tests, but didn't do well when it came to creative problem solving or thinking outside of the box for solutions.

So, in 2011, we launched the LEAP (Learning and Engaging through Access and Personalization) Initiative (eanesisd.net/leap) not only to help with those concerns, but also to increase student engagement and shift toward a personalized learning model that is student-centered and authentic.

The challenge for any school is meeting the differentiated needs of its students. Although the best 1:1 environment would be one where each student has their own teacher, technology can help solve some of this issue when done with fidelity.

We wanted students to go beyond being content consumers to constructing their own understanding and moving to a level of content creation to show evidence of learning. In surveying students and teachers in our district, we could see where the gaps were between what we were offering and how they were receiving it.

A review of survey data from 2011 to 2014 shows that students at Westlake High School consistently reported feeling more engaged in class when iPads were used. Those students indicated a mild to significant increase in engagement ranging from 80.9% to 87.2% over the three years of the study. A full 100% of students reported that they had noticed an increase in communication between teacher and student since the introduction of iPads. Distraction was a major concern at the outset of the program. Data from the spring 2012 survey showed that 54% of students felt that their device was a source of distraction. Survey data from the spring of 2014 showed that number decreasing by almost 20%.

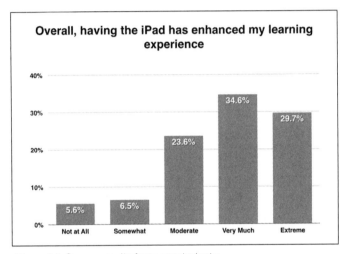

Figure 1.1 Survey results from our students.

When asked to respond to the statement "Overall, having the iPad has enhanced my learning experience," the three-year range showed that 83.5% to 87.9% of students responded with 3 (moderate) to 5 (extreme) (Figure 1.1).

I'm not sharing this data with you to brag about how we've done it, but to give you some insight into the data and thinking behind the process. Your school or district may have other reasons for doing a mobile device initiative. It might be to increase test scores in a difficult subject or to better personalize the learning experience for students. Regardless of the reason, when the process is done right, there is a lot of potential for learning and student engagement. In the end, it's hard to get a student to learn if they aren't engaged in some way.

When Mobile Learning Initiatives Fail

The number of schools embarking on some sort of mobile device initiative has increased exponentially over the years. At the same time, the myths around these initiatives have increased and, as is typical in the news, one or two bad stories can ruin it for the bunch. Take the case of the Los Angeles Unified School District (LAUSD) and their infamously failed iPad initiative. It was amazing how many messages we received from all over the country when the news broke about L.A. dropping their mobile learning program.

It's easy to go in and play Monday morning quarterback with the reasons behind the failure of the program (an article here doing that: mrhook.it/lausd), but I do applaud a district of that size for trying to innovate, even if they went about it the wrong way. As the research I described earlier points out, just throwing devices with preloaded software into the hands of kids doesn't actually create change. It still comes down to the purpose of use and the change in instructional practices from a lecture-based style to more of a student-centered model. This kind of change takes years of professional learning and administrative support to bring about.

Besides the lack of pedagogical change, another major reason why mobile learning initiatives fail is the lack of support from the community (both in and out of schools). Part of the reason why I felt so strongly about writing a parent-focused book for this series is that I have seen firsthand how powerful a supportive family can be to an initiative like ours.

When parents are informed and given resources to support the initiative from home, there is a momentous shift in perception of how the device should be used that affects learning. If the students, families, and teachers see it as a tool to leverage, the mobile device truly starts to meet its potential as a disruptive (in a good way) tool for learning.

The Digital Future of Education and the Job Market

It's difficult to predict the future of anything, much less technology. Most predictions are based on data and long-term prognostications built on research. The New Media Consortium's yearly K–12 Horizon Report is a robust report that has had a high level of accuracy over the years when it comes to predicting educational technology. The 2016 report made predictions such as cloud computing being on the "one year or less" horizon and items like the internet of things and wearable technology entering schools in the next four to five years. Locally, we also look at national and state trends with legislative direction to guide our thinking.

With national and state demands to increase the use of assessments online, districts will need to supply devices during those testing windows, because rotating through computer labs isn't feasible. Although using devices solely for testing shouldn't be the goal of an initiative, it is a value-add when you can use them instead of the paper-and-pencil or traditional computer-lab-assisted test. Like textbooks, leveraging mobile devices to help defray some costs while making learning more nimble can be a good thing.

Speaking of textbooks, the textbook market has entered a transition period of more digital text compared to hard copy. The federal government and publishers see the shift to mobile devices and tablets and are planning accordingly. In two or three years, there will be limited options in the "non-digital" market, meaning that our students will need some device to access content. The Federal Communications Commission (FCC) estimates a $3 billion dollar savings in education once that shift happens completely (and the cost of tablets continues to drop). States like Florida have adopted legislation that requires all districts to spend at least half of their instructional materials budget on digital content by 2015–16.

The future world that our students walk into will be immersed in technology and heavily influenced by social media. Besides just creating those "digital footprints" that I'll discuss in greater detail in Chapter 4, it's imperative that schools educate students in the area of digital responsibility and give them the essential skills they need in order to be good digital citizens.

The future job market for our children is also expanding, especially in the realm of computer science. In my home state of Texas, there is an enormous growth of jobs requiring some level of computer science education. When taking that growth into account, it's predicted that only 31% of jobs will be fillable with current educational models by the year 2018.

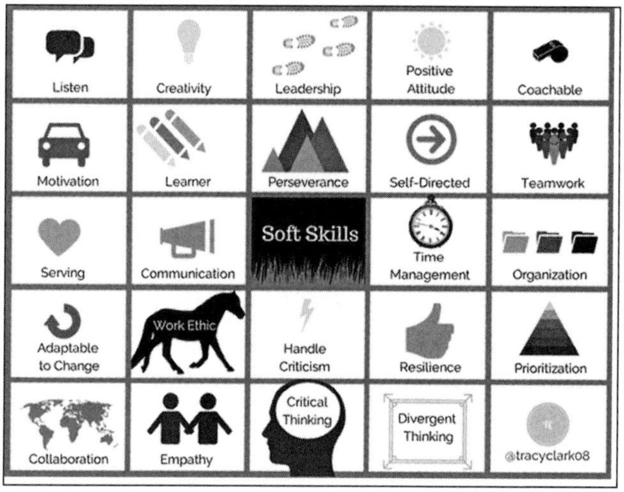

Figure 1.2 Tracy Clark's representation of what skills Fortune 500 CEOs want in future employees

So what kind of skills do employers want in future employees? One of the most powerful graphics I've seen communicate this information was from Tracy Clark's (@tracyclark08) flyer she created on Smore.com called "Measuring What Matters" (smore.com/bg57). When CEOs at *Fortune* 500 companies were asked what they want most in future employees, the words that they repeated the most were represented in her "Soft Skills Bingo" card (Figure 1.2). What stands out to me right away isn't so much what you see as what you *don't* see. I don't see "good at math" or "proficient in writing" or even "good with Microsoft Office." You see skills like perseverance, resilience, teamwork, leadership, and those 4 C's we often hear about (collaboration, communication, critical thinking, and creativity). These "future-ready" skills, as I refer to them, are much more important to the future of our kids. So shouldn't we focus on them?

CHAPTER 2

TOP 10 THINGS NOT TO DO

One of the hardest things in life is to criticize a parent. In many ways it's a step above criticizing someone's teaching style or ability, because it is extremely personal. Parenting isn't a science—it's an art form. Sometimes that art is messy, and other times it is a thing of beauty.

I often see the extremes of parenting posted all over social media, from the good ("Cindy just lost her first tooth!") to the bad ("Walked into my living room and this was what I saw—flour everywhere!") to the unreal ("Johnny just played Beethoven's First Piano Concerto at age five!"). These posts are meant to connect us and our families, but at times they can breed anxiety about our own parenting—"My kid isn't playing the piano, so does that make me a bad parent?" They can also bring about shaming or judgment—"My kid would *never* act that way in a restaurant."

We'll delve more deeply into social media in Chapter 6. But it does influence much of what we do as a parent raising a child in the digital age. Part of parenting is learning when to be loose and when to be tight with restrictions for our kids. The 10 things mentioned here are not hard-and-fast rules. Each child is different, and each circumstance can yield a different consequence, depending on the action and the pattern of behavior.

With that pretext, this list of 10 things *not* to do as a parent raising a kid in the digital age is meant to offer tools of awareness and strategy. As with the other top-10 chapters in previous books, many of these are born out of actual mistakes I've either witnessed or experienced as a parent.

1. Do *Not* Take the Device Away

This is probably the most controversial piece of advice I've ever given to parents. The knee-jerk reaction of many parents whenever a child makes a mistake is to take away the reason for the mistake. If siblings are fighting over Legos, you tell them you are going to take the Legos away until they can work it out. In the case of a toy or game, this can be an effective way to mitigate problems before they happen or get out of control.

However, in the case of mobile devices, these are not simple toys or games. These are communication devices and connections to the outside world. These are tools for learning and distraction all at the same time. When a child makes a mistake and is caught looking at an inappropriate site or having an inappropriate conversation with someone online, taking the device away will solve the issue in the short term. But it doesn't address the problem in the long term.

The easy way out is to remove the device and not discuss the issue. But this only kicks the can further down the road, and you also set the precedent of taking away the device whenever an issue arises. Put yourself in the shoes of your child: Would you be as forthcoming with an online issue or discovering something inappropriate if you knew it meant the device would be taken away? Not at all! In fact, in most cases, kids would feel more compelled to hide things from you in the future just to avoid that consequence. As I said at the beginning of this chapter, there are always unique circumstances where this may be the best option. However, try to avoid taking the device away for small infractions. Instead, turn the situation into a learning opportunity and a conduit to a more open conversation.

2. Do *Not* Assume Your Child Will Stay out of Mischief

"Oh, I have a good kid. He wouldn't get into that stuff."

I have had more than my fair share of parents tell me in confidence that, whatever indiscretion may have occurred, it couldn't possibly be *their* child. I've even had one parent who was convinced that someone else had hacked into their child's account and posted inappropriate things or performed searches for inappropriate websites.

Kids are kids. They have a natural curiosity, just like we all did when we were young (and hopefully still do to some extent). Even the most well-intentioned kid can succumb to peer pressure and end up in a situation that may be inappropriate or challenging. Because people do not have a fully formed frontal cortex until their mid-20s, younger people's judgment may be lacking at times.

Combine their lack of judgment with peer pressure, throw in some of that natural curiosity, and add mobile devices with access to information all over the world, and you could have a recipe for disaster, even with the most well-intentioned child. Although it is fine to think that your child is too well-behaved to do anything out of bounds online or with their device, don't let that lure you into a false sense of security. Continue to reinforce positive behavior while keeping one eye open for that inevitable moment when your child will encounter or search for something inappropriate.

3. Do *Not* Forget to Give Them Room to Grow

We are ultimately raising adults, not kids.

During one of the hardest periods of our mobile device initiative, I found myself in a precarious situation and was reminded of this statement. We had just finished up our first big parent night, where we went over tools and strategies for parents to use when managing mobile devices at home. At the end of the night, I was surrounded by a dozen or so angry parents who were not happy with this new burden of parenting that was seemingly being thrust upon them. I understood their frustration—but rather than try to defend it, a smile started to stretch across my face.

"Why are you smiling?" one of the parents said, "Can't you see that we're mad at you?"

I nodded. "Yes, I can tell you are angry. But the reason I'm smiling is that we are having this conversation and discussion *now*. Not after your child has left your house and headed to college to make potentially life-altering mistakes."

As hard as that moment was for many parents in the room, the fact we were discussing problems and strategies for their 13- or 14-year-old child meant their level of awareness was raised. Although not the purpose of our mobile device initiative, a positive side effect was the fact that parents and families were now acutely aware of what the future might hold for their kids going forward into the workplace or college.

Some parents took this challenge head-on and tried to restrict as much as possible on the device. In some ways, this is like not allowing your kid to drive a car until they're completely out of the house. Wouldn't you rather have them learn to drive with your assistance before they become independent of your support? Sure, that might mean the occasional dent or traffic ticket, but neither of those offenses are unrecoverable for a child. However, getting behind the wheels of a car for the first time in college without parental support or supervision could lead to greater damages and consequences. The same principle applies with mobile devices.

As hard as it is sometimes as a parent, be sure to give your child some level of freedom to explore online and be there for them when they fail or make a mistake. Being there when mistakes happen (and they will) makes a difference between whether the mistake is a failure or learning opportunity.

4. Do *Not* Forget Who Owns the Device

As I just mentioned, kids need some freedom to stretch, learn, and make mistakes, but they should never forget who the parent is when it comes to a device. Some parents have creatively figured out ways to let their teenager pay for the device or the mobile plan as a way to encourage independence and responsibility. I think this is an excellent idea, as long as it doesn't mean you give up all control of the device.

Some parents feel that they can't ask their child for their phone if there is an issue or dilemma. Kids may feel like their privacy is being invaded if you do take their phone away to look at what they are looking at. A parent once gave me some great advice about having the "privacy argument" with their child and their phone.

She told her child, "I give you privacy when you are in your bedroom changing clothes or in the bathroom. But what you post or do online is not private—therefore it shouldn't be a problem for me to look at what you are doing with your phone. If there ever is a time when I ask for your phone and you hesitate to give it to me for some reason, then you know whatever you have been doing could be considered inappropriate."

I loved her clear communication and message to her child in this scenario. It's one that can carry on with her through life, as it's true that whatever they post online can stick with them forever. Giving kids extra responsibility is good— but never forget that you ultimately own the device, and you are responsible for enforcing the rules.

Figure 2.1 My middle child's reaction when I take away her device.

Sometimes it's good to revisit the conversation about who owns the device and what privacy rights look like. It might end in a tantrum (Figure 2.1) or lead to difficult conversations, but it is necessary for establishing boundaries.

5. Do *Not* Think Parenting Today Is the Same as When You Were a Kid

Raising a child today is different from raising one a couple of decades ago. There are still some basic tenets of parents (rule-setting, boundary-setting, expectations, and so on) that will always be a part of trying to raise a child, but the playing field has shifted from a physical one to a virtual one when it comes to their lives.

Locking the doors and windows so a child can't sneak out worked fine when we were kids, but today there's a large window to the world that kids can escape through using an internet connection. This can mean more connections for kids who may be shy or for kids who don't feel like they fit into a group, but it can also mean more potential for negative interactions.

It is safe to assume that many of the guidelines and rules you were raised with can still work in today's digital age. But be prepared to adapt them for this new virtual world. Kids will still push boundaries. Maybe instead of sneaking out the window to visit a friend, they will sneak onto an online chat to have a conversation with that friend. Instead of experimenting with alcohol or drugs, they may decide to visit an inappropriate website or play a vulgar game online.

6. Do *Not* Create Rules without Input

Most household rules are put in place because of an incident or problem that may have arisen. Creating rules on the fly that are not easy to carry out can be detrimental to the growth of your child's mindset in the digital age. There is a time to put your foot down when a major problem happens, but when possible, try to share in the ownership of the decision or rule.

I'll cover this in greater detail in Chapter 8, but inviting your kids to collaborate on the household and technology rules can make those rules much more meaningful and enforceable. Whenever I employed this tactic as a classroom teacher, I found that in some cases the students were even more strict than I was. I also found that following through with the consequences was much easier because the kids self-enforced and self-regulated.

7. Do *Not* Forget to Model

At some point between the birth of my second and third child, I realized I had a bit of a problem. I was addicted to checking my phone and constantly staying updated with emails, text messages, and social media. When I came home from work (in a job where I constantly checked email, text messages, and social media), I would continue to stay "plugged in." At some point one of my kids was trying to get my attention, but I was busy checking my phone.

PARENT TOOLKIT

A "Nest" for Devices

Purpose: A centralized place to put all devices to charge before bed and help regulate too much screen time at night by keeping devices out of the bedroom.

Apps/tools: Multi-device charging stations available online or simply a power strip with charging cords plugged in.

Set-up: Find a common location (kitchen, living room) where devices will be put before going to bed. Have everyone in the family place their devices here before bedtime and leave them until in the morning.

You know it's a success when: You and your family are sleeping more soundly and not staying up until all hours of the night staring at your mini-screens.

Challenge: Some people use their phones as alarm clocks, and kids may use this as an excuse to keep their phone in their room. For $10, purchase a traditional alarm clock to help overcome this challenge.

What my actions said to my kid at that moment was that the phone was more important than them. I'd preached patience to my kids, but there I was, checking my phone when there wasn't anything important happening on it at that moment. I just couldn't escape the need for constant connection.

When we work with our kids on creating rules, we need to feel comfortable following the rules and modeling the behavior as well. Our kids take on a large part of our own personalities in life. When they see us posting rude comments on social media sites or misbehaving online, they think this must be acceptable for them, too.

The lines between work and home are now forever blurred in many ways because of the ease with which we can instantly connect. Just don't forget that at some point you must also practice what you preach and set a good example by putting away all technology at the dinner table, or plugging your phone in and not taking it to your bedroom before nighttime. Your child is observing and learning from your behavior, and you could be missing some of the most important things in life right in front of you (Figure 2.2).

Figure 2.2 The look from my youngest daughter I might have missed if I was busy checking my phone.

8. Do *Not* Assume Internet Filters Will Protect 100%

There are many great tools and resources for parents out there to help protect their kids from inappropriate content or negative interactions online. In Chapter 7, I cover a great many of these filters and restrictions that help create a "walled garden" around raising your digital child.

That said, it's important to know that if you build a 20-foot wall around your child, they will find a way to build a 21-foot ladder to get over the wall. Kids have the benefit of time and lack of responsibility. That, coupled with their curiosity, can mean there are times when they will hack their way around whatever filters or restrictions you have in place.

Although having some of these tools in place can provide some much-needed support for parenting in the digital age, it's dangerous to assume that any tool will block out all inappropriate actions and content. Filters and restrictions are not a substitute for effective parenting, and the number one most effective tool is still your two eyes. Observing your child's behavior and talking with them about why they use particular tools or sites not only can be enlightening to you as a parent—it also communicates concern and investment into whatever your child may be doing. Your non-judgmental interest in their online actions can open up other doors of dialogue and help you better understand why your child is obsessed with selfies or funny cat videos online.

9. Do *Not* Ignore the Latest Trends

Speaking of selfies, social media and technology trends can change at the drop of a hat. In 2004, Facebook was invented as a way for college kids to interact and be social online. This was not a new concept. In fact, both classmates.com and Friendster had similar services that were around well before Facebook existed.

For whatever reason, Facebook took off with teens and twenty-somethings. This is ironic because now, the population of 13- to 24-year-olds getting on Facebook has stagnated or completely fallen off. Kids are now flocking to a slew of other social media sites, which I'll cover in Chapter 6.

Why are kids trying out all of these different sites? Adults can largely look in the mirror to see the right answer. Sometime after the Facebook revolution took off, many parents and grandparents began to create accounts on the site. Kids saw this as an invasion of their social space, so they quickly left to find another space to connect away from adults. Whether they choose Twitter, Instagram, or Snapchat, kids are constantly shifting between platforms—so much so that it becomes almost commonplace for a teenager to have as many as 8 or 10 social media accounts.

Keeping up with the latest trends can help with some of this. Using a site like Common Sense Media (commonsense.org) can keep you in the loop with what kids are getting into as well as open the door to potential conversations between you and your child.

10. Do *Not* Avoid Hard Conversations

Some conversations can be hard. Much of parenting is about kids' struggle for independence and parents' need to put boundaries in place to protect them. As I mentioned in the first thing not to do, simply taking the device away can be the easiest solution, but not necessarily the right one.

Why your kid posted certain images on a social media site or why they want to visit a site that is mildly vulgar or inappropriate is not something they want to talk about. It is probably not something even you as a parent want to talk about. But by having these hard conversations with your kids in an open and non-judgmental format, you can build trust and help provide guidance when asked.

Here's an example: You notice that your child has been behaving differently lately. They aren't eating much and seem to want to avoid going to school. Although this can be caused by any number of issues related to teen angst, it could also mean that they are facing a conflict online with friends or maybe even a case of cyberbullying. Our first reaction might be to take away the social media site or cell phone that is being used as a conduit for your child's torment. However, this doesn't solve the larger problem of helping your child deal with conflict and build self-esteem.

As a child being raised with the last name "Hooker," I faced much ridicule and torment. My daughters will face many of these same issues growing up with that name. They have the same options I had when dealing with that name: Either avoid it all together and hide, or use it as a source of strength and empowerment. Sure, that sounds easy now that I'm an adult, but at the time, I remember really struggling with all the giggles and snickers whenever a teacher mentioned my name.

The truth is, all kids have some sort of challenge to overcome in life. Most bullies start out bullying other kids because they themselves are bullied. Some kids reach out to strangers online because they don't feel a part of a group at their school or in their neighborhood. There are many reasons why kids do inappropriate things in life or online, but by avoiding the hard conversations about these actions, you are robbing your child of a learning opportunity that could help them later in life.

CHAPTER 3

INTERVIEW WITH DEVORAH HEITNER

A few years ago I was doing some researching on digital parenting, and a name kept coming up. Devorah Heitner was one of the few researchers in the field who actually went into schools and spoke with students about their ideas, fears, and frustrations about being raised in the digital age.

In 2014, I had the pleasure of seeing Devorah speak at SXSWedu in Austin and came away with a load of ideas and tools to use with parents in my own community. Devorah and I have had several exchanges over the years, and I consider her one of the preeminent experts on parenting in the digital age.

Devorah Heitner

You can find out more about Devorah at her website Raising Digital Natives (raisingdigitalnatives.com) and check out her books *Connecting Wisely in the Digital Age* and *Screenwise: Helping Kids Thrive (and Survive) in Their Digital World.*

I hope you enjoy the following interview with Devorah. As with all the interviews in this series, there is a link included at the end if you want to watch the full interview online.

Carl Hooker (CH): Tell me what your current job is and how you got to this place in life. What is your origin story?

Devorah Heitner (DH): I started Raising Digital Natives in 2012. I had been a media studies professor and teaching 18- to 22-year-old undergrads about media studies, and my favorite class was Kids' Media Culture. We would go out to American Girl and all kinds of toy stores and arcades to learn about kids media, TV, and game design. What I recognized with kids and media is that kids and adolescents were using more and more interactive technologies, and the adults in their lives (teachers, parents) seemed more stressed and confused about the ways kids were creating their own communities in these spaces. So I founded Raising Digital Natives to help parents and educators understand how kids were using technology and to better understand how to mentor them as they grow up in the digital age and in an interactive space.

CH: Wow! It's interesting, but as you were talking, I was thinking about all the changes that have happened over our lifetime or even the lifetime of my own kids. But this is not a new thing. I would say that parents in the '50s and '60s were probably a little upset about television and the mobile radio. But you're right—technology has kind of spurred on this whole new era of concern and worry, which, in some ways is good, because if they aren't concerned or at least thinking about it, then that's a problem. You mention you've done research. When and where have you done research for your books and your website?

DH: A lot of the research comes from when I do workshops with kids. I'm learning from them as they are learning from me. But I've also done focus groups that were not paid workshops, just times when I would come in and ask kids, for example, what are the things that stress you out about being connected? What are the things that you love about being connected? What's it like being an 11-year old with a smartphone? What's it like being a 14-year-old who doesn't have one in a community where it's the norm to get one? What are some conflicts that come up in online gaming situations? What's so fun about group texting? Why does every sixth grader like to group text so much—or at least it seems that way to parents and educators. And for the kids who abstain—you know you meet kids in every community that may say "I'm actually not on Instagram" or "I'm choosing not to do social media"—what's in it for them? What do they get out of *not* doing it? What are the kids who are super users getting out of it?

These are the kinds of questions that get kids talking, and a lot of kids will say [things like} "Adults worry so much about what I'm doing on there but they don't really know what I'm doing," or "I'm really glad you asked about Minecraft—let me tell you about it," or "I'm really glad you asked about Snapchat stories or musical.ly—let me show you what I'm doing." I find that once I get a group of kids talking about their experiences using interactive games or learning to program, they are very eager to explain what is exciting about it. They also have their own critiques about maybe some of the negative things that other kids have done, or things that they have seen that they don't like. So I don't think that kids are these uncritical users of technology. I've seen, certainly in the edtech space, where kids are critical edtech, bad apps, or the times where educators aren't using technology in the best or most productive ways that really support student learning. You know what? The kids know.

CH: Yes! I had a parent his past year call it "gratuitous tech," meaning it was using tech for tech's sake, like taking selfies for fun. I've seen selfies used productively in a challenge, too, but I understand where they are coming from. I remember a story you shared at SXSW when you mentioned an 11-year-old getting frustrated with a friend for not responding to a text right away. It seems that sixth grade is the year most kids in my community are getting cell phones, so I wonder if you could shed some light on that when it comes to empathy?

DH: There are some positive things—kids can start to have more independence maybe, traveling around the community, and the parents feel like that is a safe connection. But I think there are some challenges. One of them is that kids that age are quite impatient socially, and they haven't had a lot of experiences having to manage their emotions on their own around these things, because they are doing so many supervised playdates or organized activities. Kids are having to cultivate their patience and these other kinds of etiquette and emotional resilience that you need in such a connected world. Because it's possible to be connected all the time, they expect others will be as well. When they're not, they get irate. I've even had college students get irate with me as a professor if I didn't respond to their emails at 4 in the morning on a Sunday about something that had been on the syllabus for six weeks.

CH: *(laughs)*

DH: I think it's very important for kids to recognize that there is another human being on the other end of that phone, and she may be eating dinner, or playing basketball, or not allowed to text after 8 o'clock. We shouldn't have a panic attack when someone doesn't respond to us right away. Try to imagine some scenarios where [someone] may be busy or disconnected and that's OK. If we don't hear from them in a couple of days, we can check back in, right? We really have to manage that expectation, and parents can model that by saying, like I say to my son, "I'm going to text Dad right now, but I know he's at work—so if he's in a meeting, we might not hear back from him right away."

CH: Yes, and with the wearables entering the world, that means notifications are attached to you in some ways. And it's not just kids. Sometimes I'll get a phone call or text from an adult asking me "Hey, did you see that email I just sent?" So I think you need to model, too, you're right.

We are running a 1:1 device program and that's what a lot of this book is about. With that comes some concerns from parents who are fearful of technology and don't want their kids to use it, but now the school has issued it. What advice would you have for school leaders who are wrestling with that scenario?

DH: You don't want to throw kids into the deep end. To send a kid into college or the job market without experience, for example, collaboratively editing a document or writing an appropriate email to seek information is actually irresponsible in this day and age. You are setting that person up to be at a huge disadvantage because other people will have those skills. So I'm not going to argue with you that you *must* know this certain program, but I will say—some basic keyboarding skills, basic communication, and etiquette via email. Email is still critically important in the work world and in colleges. So kids need that absolutely. They also need some collaboration skills on digital documents, because that's the way the world is working. So just some of those very basic skills are important.

A lot of folks are arguing for computer science and coding everywhere. I do think that coding is an important literacy. I wouldn't say personally that every kid needs to be a proficient coder and that they would be in trouble if they are not.

CH: I agree.

DH: I don't think that's the job market and world right now, but maybe at some point. I do think for kids to be exposed to it—maybe they aren't fully literate in it, but they kind of know how the apps they use work—would be a good idea. These are some of the literacies that kids need. We also need to think about what we are replacing and make some smart decisions. We do want kids who, if their smartphone battery dies, know how to ask someone for directions. We want kids to have all those "old world" skills along with these wonderful new skills.

Parents are afraid because they see the internet as this threatening place. It's not curated for kids, and parents are not wrong to be worried about the content that is out there. It is much better to be guided at school in terms of what to do when you encounter an inappropriate site, rather than receive no guidance. The same can be said in terms of what you share. If you take a high school kid and just drop him into the "digital deep end," he's at a disadvantage compared to the child that has spent time learning what's appropriate or inappropriate to share. How do you handle an inappropriate comment on your blog post? How do you solve that conflict?

I would much rather kids learn to share in these "micro-public" settings, like a school or classroom, rather than learn to share in the global public of YouTube or Twitter. These are places that are very searchable, and the older you are, the more your mistakes are held against you. It's much better to learn those mistakes on a semi-private blog as a 9-year-old rather than in a very open forum as a 16-year-old.

CH: Do you sense there is a shift where kids today are getting smarter or more aware of their profiles online?

DH: I think kids are more aware of the harm, but I think it's our role as adults to desensitize the stigma and shame around digital mistakes. We need to work toward a climate of repair in terms of moving forward and having grace, which includes not letting kids heap on the shame and stigma of other kids' mistakes. And we need to make sure that other kids also have grace and don't shame the kid that made the mistake online. Oftentimes they made the same mistake, but just didn't get caught. We've all made digital mistakes.

The other thing we need to discuss with kids is how to handle an online conflict with someone. Sometimes those conflicts can't be resolved in a discussion thread and need to be handled either face to face or with a phone call. You can't always resolve those with a text. Once things go awry in the digital space, it's very hard to get back that human quality using digital means.

CH: That [was] never more evident than during the 2016 presidential election. One only needs to get on Facebook to see some of this in action, and as adults, we don't always model the best or ideal behavior when interacting with conflict online.

Speaking of digital shaming, I mention a young lady later in this book who made the poor choice to dress up as a Boston Marathon bombing victim. Her posting of it was in absolute poor taste, but in some ways the shaming and harassment that followed her online was far worse—talk about killing her parents, and just some evil statements meant to really shame her. That's a good point to mention to kids—that it's easy to heap on, but sometimes it's best to take the high road.

Changing subjects a bit here, but where do you go to be inspired?

DH: Well, it depends. I'm lucky enough to live close to Lake Michigan, so I'm close to the beach. I also swim laps at the Y.

CH: Not in Lake Michigan? *(laughs)*

DH: No, I don't swim my laps in Lake Michigan. It's pretty cold. Maybe by August. *(laughs)*

CH: Wow! You are brave!

DH: Definitely in the water is where I get inspiration. I also get a lot of inspiration from the kids I work with. Kids will create solutions for problems, and some of the most inventive and innovative ideas I've heard from kids. Kids are great problem solvers, and they haven't put up the walls or blinders like some of us adults do. I see 10- and 11-year-olds just dive into a problem and in 45 minutes come up with some pretty inventive solutions. So I find that pretty inspiring.

CH: They aren't as inhibited by our structures and limitations as adults.

DH: Absolutely.

CH: What is something that parents should be worried about that they are not currently?

DH: That's a great question. I think "exclusion" is a problem with social media. It's easy for a kid to live on the margins and not feel like their life is as good as everyone else's lives. It's also easy to quantify your popularity based on how many friends or likes you have. The reality is you can really only have a limited amount of close friends, so if you have 600 acquaintances online, that doesn't necessarily equate to friendship.

Another thing is that in the age of Google and Siri, kids are somewhat critical of their sources. I don't want kids to be total skeptics, but I do want them to consider sources and consider bias. It helps that my husband is a journalist and we are very involved in those conversations in our house all the time.

Where does information come from? If it's free, then someone is paying for that information—what does that look like? I see a lot of adults circulating articles on Facebook of dubious quality, which makes you wonder—they are critiquing kids using Google for everything, yet they post something that has some really big holes in it from an information or journalistic perspective. So just thinking about source quality and for kids to be critical consumers of information and critical of their own privacy, like, "Who am I going to give that data to and why?"

As a Gen X-er I'm very protective of my privacy, but I've seen with Millennials and Gen Z-ers that's not the case. Kids will say it's better to be safe than private. They aren't that concerned with privacy, and I think we should all be concerned with that.

So those are some things that I think [parents should] cultivate their own literacy about. And ultimately, balance. Are they modeling a balanced use of tech in their own lives? They yell at their kid to get off their computer, but they are staring at their phone all day?

CH: Speaking of privacy—while I was writing this book, the Pokémon GO phenomenon was happening around the country, which really calls into question the use of privacy. Their initial document allowed for a ton of data tracking. Sometimes we need to look into what data are we giving up before we opt in.

DH: Yes. Some friends of mine created spam Google accounts just to use for things like that.

CH: A good suggestion and practice when giving up data for sure. So we talked about things that parents should be worrying about but aren't—but what about the opposite? What are some things that parents are way too concerned with but shouldn't be?

DH: I think parents are way too worried about screen time, probably more than they should be. Because of some old statements by the American Association of Pediatrics, I think parents sometimes get obsessed with the idea of screen time and it makes them upset about what the kids are doing in school with screens. If you kid is coding or working on a Google Doc in school, it's not like they are sitting there watching something mindless.

Parents should really look at what are the screens facilitating? What kind of learning? What kind of interaction? What kind of collaboration are the screens facilitating? Yes, we should all be critical if your kid is being handed an iPad to, heaven forbid, shut them up and stick them in the corner—that would be a problem.

CH: Yes!

DH: But that's not the case in most schools and classrooms. It is iPads and Chromebooks and other types of interactive tools. Tablets are being use in much more thoughtful ways. So I'm not saying we shouldn't be critical, but screen time is something parents worry about too much, and they feel guilty. What the guilt does is keep them from talking to other parents. It can affect people differently, and a mom might think, "Oh, well—my kid got screen time today, so I'm a failure as a mom." Sure, letting them just watch YouTube videos for 12 hours a day might not be your A-game as a parent, but we all may need to do that once in a while for survival.

There are also so many cool things your kids could be doing. They could be creating their own shows. They could be watching shows that other kids and adults have created. They could be watching experiments. They could be making movies. They could be making artwork and sharing it.

Some are also concerned about their kids having a digital footprint, and they don't want teachers to share. But who better to decide what to share? Ninety-nine percent of the time, your kid's teacher will make better decisions than your kid in terms of what to share. Why not have that guidance? The teacher isn't going to share embarrassing things—she's going to share student work. It's good to have your kid's work out there even if your second grader's essay has a spelling mistake. That's not going to hurt their digital footprint. [Parents should be] looking at their child's digital portfolio as a snapshot of where that student is in their learning.

Also, don't discount your own wisdom as a parent. You have years of experience, and you know that if your kid is walking away from an app frustrated and angry, maybe it is negative for them. If it seems to energize them and is positive for friendships, and if they are able to have some balance with it and do other things like skateboard or go out running around the neighborhood killing zombies, like my kid likes to do—

CH: Or finding Pokémon—

DH: Exactly! Then I think it's a very positive thing.

CH: For those of you reading ahead to the chapter on screen time, Devorah hit on many of those points here. It's not so much about the screen time as it is the content on the screens and how they interact with it. You mentioned something that was a small point but also important—and that is, as a parent, to follow up with questions. Even if your kid is just watching a TV show or cartoon, it's good to be involved and ask the kid what they thought about the show, or ask them what they got out of it. Even that little bit of interaction can make that connection so much more powerful.

DH: Exactly!

CH: Or like my daughter who will watch an hour of Minecraft videos and I'll wonder what she's doing, but when I approach her about it, she's actually watched the videos and applied it to a creation.

DH: Right, and you definitely have to look at each kid. My kid will sort of turn into a monster after a certain amount of time doing various digital pursuits. We try and space it out throughout the day. So his total amount of weekend screen time might be two hours—but it's not all in one sitting, because that does make him into a monster, and I don't want to live with that monster.

I think we really have to look at our kids. During one of my talks I had a parent approach me with four kids and tell me she couldn't really individualize to that degree. So I say to that parent, sometimes you have to create household rules around your most sensitive customer. Or if there are some older siblings that want to play a game with some sensitive content, maybe they have to wait until the younger siblings aren't around before they do that.

CH: That's fair.

DH: You all have to work together to create an environment that works for everyone.

CH: I was going to ask you about your top three tips for parents, but I'm going to hold off on that and do a little rapid fire, then we'll follow up with those tips, OK?

DH: Awesome!

CH: So we are going to go James Lipton-style here. First thought that comes to your mind. So first question—What's a word or sound that you hate to hear?

DH: Oh my gosh, my kid screaming!

CH: *(laughs)* I'll agree with that one. What is something that gives you pride?

DH: I feel like all of these will be about my kid.

CH: Your kid not screaming?

DH: No—my husband and I have not gifted him with any athletic ability, but he just decided he wanted to master baseball, and he has just worked so hard. Even though it doesn't come to him naturally, he's really worked so hard at it, and he's improved so much since the beginning of the summer.

CH: What's the coolest thing you have in your office?

DH: I have books written by people I know, and I think that's pretty cool.

CH: I would agree—I have a few of those as well, including yours.

DH: And I'm going to have your book.

CH: If you could have dinner with any person in history, who would it be and why?

DH: I think I would go with the activist Ella Baker. I've always been a big fan of hers.

CH: Oooh. Good one. What's something that needs to be invented that hasn't?

DH: Another good question. I would say a much smarter money tracker. Like it keeps track of how you spend throughout the day. So like as I'm purchasing my lunch at Whole Foods, how exactly is that affecting my long-term projections.

CH: When was the last time you sang, and what was the song?

DH: I go to services about once a month. I'm in a little do-it-yourself Jewish community, so I'm sure I sang on Saturday because I went to services. I think I sang a song about basically beating the swords into plowshares. We've all been upset about recent violence in the country and around the world, so we sang that song. It was in Hebrew, so the words would be hard to translate, but basically that's what it was about. It made us feel good, and I think that singing is a great way to be in community with other people.

CH: I've asked that question of every interviewee, and that seems to be a common thread. Singing brings people together, but also makes people feel better. So let's wrap this up with your top three tips for parents when it comes to digital parenting.

DH: You are the model. Your relationship with technology. If you are stressed or nervous about it, remember that translates to your child.

Next, I'd say mentorship over monitoring is huge. I think if a few parents could share that thought with other parents—it's not about putting a chip in your kid's brain to track every thought they have or every text they have. It's not about a one-and-done conversation. It should be a one-on-one ongoing conversation about mentorship. And it shouldn't just be about tech, but that's part of the conversation.

And then empathy is my third tip, and it just sort of relates to those values. Always remember that there's someone else on the other side. Whether you are posting to Instagram and 300 people see it or if you are sending a little chat message to your one friend in a game, remember there is a human being on the other side of that conversation. You should be thinking, "Oh, is this something I should share? Am I adding to this relationship by sharing this? And if so, am I sure this is going to come through properly? Is my tone going to be OK?"

It's really important that we think about the people on the other side of our communication.

CH: Thank you so much! She is Devorah Heitner. And how can people get in touch with you if they want more information or to have you as a speaker?

DH: Sure! You can reach me at my website (raisingdigitalnatives.com) or email me at devorah@raisingdigitalnatives.com. And my two books are both available for order on Amazon. I'm always happy to talk to educational leaders or parents about the conversations we should be having around tech. I'm always interested in learning and having conversations around things you are experiencing and how is that adding to our lives. Thank you so much for having me!

CH: And thank you for all your work in helping parents raise digital natives!

CHAPTER 4

MAINTAINING DIGITAL WELLNESS

Balance.

Balance is a great word, and something to strive for—but know that it might never happen. No one has complete balance in their life. But we tend to have problems when that balance is out of whack. Lack of balance between work and home life. Lack of balance between diet and exercise. Lack of balance between being connected and having time to unplug. These are all struggles of the modern family, as they were in some way for families decades ago.

Today we have many more things competing for our interest and time than just each other. There are scheduled playdates, sporting events, TV shows that we have backlogged on our DVR, and the black hole that is funny cat videos on YouTube. With all of these items and more competing for our time and attention, maintaining balance in the modern age seems to be a struggle in futility.

Digital wellness is the idea that you have some level of balance between the screen and the real world. There are days when things can be out of balance because you have a paper to write or major video project to work on that requires you to stare at a screen for hours. There are other times when a funny social media discussion may occupy hours of your day or night and you aren't even aware of it. While you may be out and about with friends, you are still somewhat connected to the drama unfolding on Facebook.

Reflecting on Your Family Practices

As I mentioned in Chapter 2, on things *not* to do as a parent of a digital kid, do not forget to model the desired behavior. This can be more challenging than for kids—we may feel a need to stay connected because of work, or perhaps some distant family drama. Regardless of the reason, it's easy for adults to slip into the bad behavior of checking phones at the dinner table despite there being household rules against that very thing.

In Chapter 8, I explore how digital wellness plays a role in the household and how families can create guidelines for trying to reach balance in that area. And while the examples and strategies listed in this chapter are geared toward our kids, don't forget that idea of modeling the thing you want to see.

What follows here are modern challenges that have come about from the proliferation of mobile devices into the world. As with anything I mention throughout this book, many of these challenges or annoyances are things that I have either personally experienced or participated in. Although there is no direct prescription that will cure many of these issues, being aware goes a long way in striving for that balance.

"Nocialization"

One of the advantages to having mobile devices is the idea that we can be connected to anyone around the world at a moment's notice. With the touch of a button, we can find friends and family and keep up to date with their latest news. Social media does in fact make us more social in some ways, because we are connecting with others so effortlessly.

However, that comes at a cost. One of the side effects of the constant connection online is that when we venture out to socialize in the real world, we sometimes become addicted and are even comforted by the known connection that exists on our phones. This is especially the case when we're faced with an uncomfortable situation like the awkward silence on an elevator. In the pre-mobile era, this meant you just had to stand there and stare at the wall in uncomfortable silence. Now you have the comfort of your phone and the connections it offers as a way to cover up the awkwardness and have your body language and actions say, "Hey, I'm important, and I have stuff to do on this phone."

Although this scenario is now somewhat excusable and commonplace, there is another trend that happens with young people (and adults at times) where they go to social settings physically and choose to plug into their network rather than talk. "Nocialization" is a word that has become popularized by pop culture (mrhook.it/nocial) to describe the action of going out to a social setting and then not being social (Figure 4.1).

Part of striving toward digital wellness is being aware of these moments of nocialization and then combatting it by not joining the others in your group connecting online. One of the most common excuses given for participating in this concept is the fear of missing out (or "FOMO") on something happening online. Some people suffer from this so much that they never leave their homes in case something crazy or funny happens online—they want to make sure they are part of it while it's happening. When we get to Chapter 8, be sure to think about how you would handle this situation in your own household, and what rules you could put in place to help strive for balance between real world and virtual socialization.

Figure 4.1 Nocialization happening at the dinner table with friends.

The Digital Yawn

Do you ever have that moment where you experience something and are somewhat annoyed by it? Better yet, have you ever participated in something and ended up annoyed at yourself?

I'm one of those people who feels naked without their phone. I used to think I was in the minority, but after discussions with hundreds of adults and students, I think I'm now just part of the "in" crowd. The other day, I was with a group of colleagues discussing work life and talking some mild business when it happened again.

That moment.

I was witnessing something I sensed was happening more and more in social circles (even in non-social ones). Here's how it goes:

Everyone is standing or sitting around, having conversation, when someone decides it's time to check his phone. Maybe it vibrated. Maybe it flashed or blinked with some sort of notification, but he checked it. Then, almost without fail, someone else in the group decides to do the same thing. Only, they likely weren't notified or "pinged" for any reason. They were merely mimicking the action of a group member. Or maybe they took his action as an opportunity to break from normal social interaction to check their own device.

Only it doesn't stop there. A third person takes this opportunity to check their device. Then a fourth. Then a fifth. Eventually everyone is checking their phones. This almost involuntary reaction is what I call the "digital yawn." I wanted to call it something more viral, like YouTuberculosis or iFluenza, or maybe Cell Phonic Plague. But since it usually isn't a permanent or long-lasting event, I went with something simpler but just as contagious.

The second event that usually follows a group digital yawn is a moment of involuntary silence. This is the "nocialization" event described in the previous section. Although as a society we are becoming more and more connected, that connection comes with a cost—the cost of giving up face-to-face time with others. The cost of being fully in the moment.

So what does all this mean? Are we all becoming digital zombies? Drawn to our phones like the shuffling undead looking for brains? Are more and more of us ambling about through the world slowly as we check our text messages?

I don't think so. The reality is that, as with any innovation or cultural nuance, society is quick to become addicted and latch on. But eventually we level out. As with anything else, I believe this pendulum will swing to center. Becoming aware of these social (or non-social) situations is the first step to achieving that word mentioned at the beginning of this chapter, balance.

So the next time you are in a crowd of friends or trapped in an elevator with a bunch of strangers, resist the temptation to grab that device and check it. When you are out with your kids and feel the need to connect online, resist. When your own kids want to just plug in for that 3-hour road trip, try and get them to resist, even if only for a few minutes. Resistance may seem futile, but necessary to try and achieve balance.

A Diet on Oversharing

We all have that friend. You know the one. The one who likes to share nearly every life moment on social media. They're posting pictures of their favorite food on Instagram, or sharing pictures of their feet at almost every beach they travel to. Social media can be a great place to share life experiences, but it can also be a place to overindulge in sharing.

I sometimes think of Facebook as the great "anecdote killer." I'll have a moment when I'm meeting with friends or family for the first time in many months and I'm excited to share some of the great places we've been or some of the struggles we've overcome. Then it happens. I get cut off mid-sentence.

Me: "Last summer, the kids and I went on this road trip to—"

Friend: "Oh! You mean when you went to Disneyland? We saw that on Facebook! It looked great!"

Other times, people I haven't spoken to in years will come up and start a conversation with me as if we were just talking on the phone the day before.

Friend: "How's your dad doing?"

Me: "What?"

Friend: "I saw that someone tagged you in a post about him being in the hospital and needing prayers for his return to health."

In the second scenario, I didn't even share the information on social media. Someone else did and tagged me, which then made it available to all my friends and followers. It seems that even monitoring my own oversharing can only start to stave off the anecdote killing power of social media.

As with any negative, there are also positives. This power of instant sharing and calling for support can be used to turn the tide in elections (as we've seen in the United States) or even to get a discount due to an airline mishap (as I share in this post here: http://mrhook.it/power and Figure 4.2). However, know that there are times to keep private moments private. We need to not only model that but also discuss it with our kids.

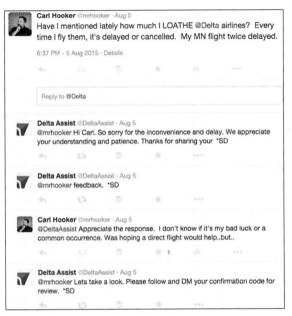

Figure 4.2 The power of social media pressure.

It's one thing to make a bad decision. It's another thing to then choose to share that bad decision online and publish it to the masses.

Take the cautionary tale of Alicia Ann Lynch. Ms. Lynch thought it would be clever to dress up as a Boston Marathon bombing victim for Halloween in 2014. It had only been a few months since the actual attack. Her choice of a costume was pretty tasteless, but her decision to pose and post pictures of it on Instagram were completely thoughtless. (More on her tale here: mrhook. it/lynch. She ended up losing her job and received multiple death threats as a result of her poor decisions that day.

I share this tale with students all the time, and although many say, "Oh, I would never do that," I'm often surprised to search their names and see what they do decide to post on social media. Oversharing can affect digital foot-prints, which we will discuss in greater detail in Chapter 10. In the case of Ms. Lynch, her digital footprint is now permanently affected, as anyone who searches her name on the internet will see article after article showcasing her poor decision.

"Notifistraction" Disease

Since the beginning of time, humans have had an innate sense of alertness. In primitive times, that's what prepared us for danger. Imagine you're hunting and gathering when you happen upon a pond with fresh water. You bend over to fill a jug, and suddenly you hear a twig snap! You turn, expecting to see a bloodthirsty beast, but it turns out to be a smaller creature—maybe a squirrel (Look! Squirrel!).

So you travel cautiously back to your cave. When you arrive home to your wife and kids, you discover that you left your jug full of water behind. "What were you thinking?" your annoyed wife asks.

The truth is, you were distracted. Your brain refocused attention and energy toward survival and alertness. In that moment, you forgot the water jug and simply returned home. The equivalent in modern times is going into a room to look for your glasses, but then something else catches your eye, and you forget why you went into the room in the first place. By our very nature, we are prone to distraction. It's what causes our brain to alter its original course of action when a new stimulus is produced.

Enter the era of smartphones, wearables, and school devices that beep and tweet, causing us to lose focus constantly. I call this "notifistraction" (no-ti-fah-strak-shun) disease. Despite our best efforts to focus, our brains still revert back to that Stone-Age, twig-snapping event whenever our devices alert us about something.

The good news is there are some simple cures available. What follows are some very basic "prescriptions" to help students—and you—better manage the constant stream of distractions.

Turn off notification alerts. I've turned off all audio alerts except text messages and phone calls. Although this might not seem like much, it helps. At one point I was getting Yelp alerts from friends visiting a new restaurant, in Sydney, Australia. Do I really need to know that?

Don't respond to everything right away. Just because you can respond to text messages, Snapchats and email quickly doesn't mean you should. Give it a break occasionally and don't respond immediately. In some cases, your lack of response will reduce the distractions coming your way and allow you to focus on your tasks.

Employ the "pomodoro technique." The word *pomodoro* is Italian for "tomato." You might be thinking, what does an Italian tomato have to do with helping with distractions? It actually refers to a tomato-like egg timer that is often used with cooking. This is a great way to focus on important projects and single-task. Here's how it works: You write down a goal or project that you need to work on. Then turn off all notifications, shut down email, and turn off your phone for 25 or 30 minutes. When the time is up, take a 5-minute break to check email, look at social media, put your clothes in the washing machine, and so on. When break time is over, set the timer for another 25 minutes and start over. In the parent toolkit box below, I share an app that I use regularly (including while writing this book) to help with this.

Stand up and go outside. When all else fails, sometimes we just have to go back to our primitive roots and walk outside for some fresh air (without our phones). The extra oxygen will awaken and alert your brain, allowing you to refocus on whatever task or project you are working on. In the classroom, using brain breaks like those provided by GoNoodle (gonoodle.com) create movement, refresh the eyes, and get the brain focused again.

Give yourself time for reflection. With all the constant connection and interaction, it's sometimes hard to think. It's almost like your brain becomes a junk drawer of items that needs to be organized or dumped every so often. I find that taking even 2 to 5 minutes every day to reflect, think, and set goals can help make me more productive and less distracted throughout the day. In the classroom, this could be as simple as having students write in a journal, or turning off the lights and letting kids sit and just think about their day. This activity can center students and help them set goals and reflect on challenges ahead. At home this might mean spending 5 minutes quietly in your room reflecting on the day.

Let's face it—we've been distracted creatures for thousands of years, but it's time we started managing those distractions. The next time you suffer from notifistraction disease, ask yourself if it's really necessary to be alerted when the washing machine is done. If not, start opting out of alerts. You might find yourself being distracted by more pleasant things, like nature and birds and … squirrels!

The constant fight for balance in this new highly distracted and digital world can seem like a battle with yourself and your kids, but it doesn't necessarily have to be. Becoming aware of some of the issues outlined in this chapter and employing some of the solutions mentioned will help you and your family move toward a healthy level of digital wellness that doesn't completely inhibit their digital and actual lives.

PARENT TOOLKIT

Single-tasking Focus and the Pomodoro Technique

Purpose: Help your child focus on one activity or project at a time as well as organize and prioritize their day.

Apps/tools: 30/30 app (3030.binaryhammer.com), timer app on your phone, or egg timer.

Setup: Assist your child in prioritizing and organizing their list of items they need to accomplish. Estimate the amount of time to complete or work on a project. Using the 30/30 app or a timer, turn off all other distractions (social media, TV, phones) and work on a single task for as long as the timer is set. After 20 or 30 minutes, build in a 5-minute break to check social media, text, stretch, and so on. Repeat until the project or task is finished.

You know it's a success when: Your child is setting their own goals and prioritizing tasks that need to be finished. When they work on a project, they aren't distracted and can focus on the project until a break. After their break they are able to re-engage and complete the work effectively and successfully.

CHAPTER 5

SCREEN TIME AND THE BRAIN

When television became popular in the middle of the 20th century, TVs were manufactured with cathode ray tubes as the source of light emission. With these tubes comes a small level of radiation. The level of radiation is relatively harmless, but still the urban legend grew that if you sat too close to the television, you would go blind or get cancer.

These legends may seem silly in retrospect, but at a time of new innovation, they were (and in some ways still are) a major concern, especially when it came to raising kids. Flash forward a few decades and we are all carrying around smaller screens in our pockets. Although these don't use cathode ray tubes for light sources (and thus there is no radiation), there is still concern and worry over the number of screens our children's brains are accessing on a regular basis.

From television to computers to smartphones to tablets to smart watches, the number of screens we now have access to has grown exponentially. What effect do all these screens have on our brain? What is the right age for kids to have access to digital screens? How much time should they spend on a screen at any one time?

These are all questions that I encounter both as a parent and as an administrator of a 1:1 school district. The real answer is … it depends.

More on that in a moment, but first let's take a look at what the American Academy of Pediatrics (AAP) recommends and how their own recommendations have evolved quickly over time as the pace of technology growth (and screens) continues to increase all around us.

Research on Screen Time

Common Sense Media did a survey in 2015 of tweens and teens and how much time they spent on various media platforms. The results (posted here in a great infographic: mrhook.it/screentime) showed some surprising trends and some that were not so surprising.

First, boys tended to be gamers more than girls, and girls tended to lean more toward social platforms like Instagram and Snapchat than boys did. What was surprising was the amount of time kids spent looking at a screen. The average tween (8 to 12 years old) spends around 4 1/2 hours a day looking at a screen in some form or fashion. The average teenager (13 to 18 years old) spends more than 6 1/2 hours a day looking at screens (Common Sense Media, 2015).

What exactly are they looking at, and how do they have time in the day for all of that? Most kids in the survey claim to be able to multitask throughout the day. This means they can be watching TV while checking their social media stream, which essentially doubles the number of screens they are watching each minute. Although a large percentage of screen time is dedicated to passive watching of media (videos, TV, reading), there has been an increase in the use of screens for interactive applications (as with gaming) and communication (as with social media).

Why does any of this matter? It turns out that in the most recent release of the AAP recommendations for screen time, they stopped lumping all screen interaction into one single category. Rather than doing that, they have adapted their policies and suggestions to address more the content and level of interaction with the media (mrhook.it/update). Whereas their old recommendations break down the ages of kids into subgroups, the new recommendations tend to be in two categories: Kids below the age of 2 and kids above the age of 2 (Shapiro, 2015).

It's true—the brain is constantly forming and evolving. Overexposure to anything (bad food, alcohol, tobacco, or questionable media) can be bad for a developing brain. In our modern world, we are constantly surrounded by screens. From the supermarket to our car, screens are vying for our attention and the attention of our kids. Just as I mentioned in the previous chapter on digital wellness, we should be striving for balance in our kids use of screen time.

Screen Time: How Much, When, What?

So when is it OK to indulge in screen time? Or is it ever a good idea? The truth is that it depends. It depends on the content being viewed. It depends on how the child is interacting with the content. It depends on what kind of involvement the parent has with the media as well.

Content

In the case of content being viewed, you want to set limits on things that children can't quite comprehend. Violence, sex, drugs, and other inappropriate forms of content are generally best to avoid at early ages. Notice that I'm not mentioning a specific age, because it honestly could depend on the child. I have three children, and each one of them is different in terms of how they handle content. My oldest child was able to differentiate reality from nonreality in a movie like *Jurassic Park* (although I did skip the T-rex scene). My middle child would be convinced that the dinosaurs in that film are outside walking around if I showed it to her at the same age.

The content rating system in the United States is fairly broad for a reason. There are times when a piece of content might be best served with parental guidance and other times when we should restrict anyone below the age of 17 from viewing it. I've already mentioned Common Sense Media (commonsensemedia.org) and will likely mention them many more times in this book because I feel they are a great resource for parents looking for what's appropriate and what isn't when it comes to content. A great movie that you may have watched as a kid might not really be appropriate for a 9-year-old nowadays. Regardless, remember that each child is different. These are not hard and fast rules, but rather guidelines for looking at what content is appropriate and what content isn't.

Interactive versus Passive

One of the greatest experiences of being involved in a mobile learning initiative from the beginning is seeing the evolution of how the screen is used in a classroom. Before our own 1:1, a lot of money was spent on giant interactive whiteboards with projectors. The focus of the lesson and control of the technology was all in the hands of the teacher. As the movement toward tablets and less expensive laptops has begun to infiltrate classrooms, the need for giant screens to focus students' attention also has changed.

As a first grade teacher in the early 21st century, I would often "borrow" the one projector we had in our school so that I could display graphics and images in a large, visually pleasing manner. Students could sit back and consume whatever I was showing them as I hoped it passively would enter their brain.

A couple of years later, we received a set of Apple iBooks on a cart (affectionately called CoW—Computers on Wheels). I noticed a marked difference in students' behavior as well as engagement when I quit using the big screen and let them use and control their own little screen. They were instantly more engaged in the project and seemed to remember much more of the content than before.

Figure 5.1. My day as a substitute involved students interacting and moving with an app called Nearpod.

The difference? They were actually moving and interacting with the content, rather than just passively absorbing it (Figure 5.1). When it comes to your own child and their use of screen time, try and estimate how much of their screen time is active versus passive. Neuroscience research has discovered that the brain is actually more active during sleep than when passively watching a television show. (It's even less active when watching reality television.) However, brainwaves tend to spike more often when interacting with a touchscreen or mouse. Mobilizing the action of the learning means that a student actually has more brain activity, which in turn helps with learning outcomes and objectives.

The Role of the Parent

Screen time can be either an interactive or passive sport. It can involve content that is appropriate or inappropriate. One of the largest difference makers in the effect of screen time isn't the content or interactivity, though—it's relational.

When a parent sits down with a child to watch a movie or show together or to play a game, it creates a shared experience. This shared experience can lead to things like questions about a scenario playing out on a TV show, or problem-solving a strategy to win a video game. Regardless of outcome, simply being present with a child during a session of screen time can have extremely positive effects on their experiences with what they are watching or interacting with.

Taken to the next level, think about this scenario. You observe your child playing on their phone and possibly interacting with someone on a social media site that you aren't familiar with. You have a couple of options at this point. You can get involved and ask them what they are doing out of your own interest and to show your concern, or ignore their actions and just figure they are "kids being kids." Either of these actions can set in motion a wide range of outcomes based, not on the screen interaction of the kid and their device, but rather your interaction with the kid and their device.

Simply showing an interest in their actions and asking innocent questions like "Can you show me how this works?" gives the child the opportunity to be an expert to some extent. They can explain to you what it is they are doing, who they are communicating with, and why they are using the tool. This also opens up a conversation in which you can ask further questions like, "Why would someone post that?" or "I wonder who all can see that?" Your kid may be an expert with the technology, but you hold something greater than their techno-expertise: wisdom. The wisdom that comes with years of trial and error. Wisdom they can only gain over time and through conversations with others that may have traveled a similar path in some ways.

All of these opportunities to share and discuss with your child would be lost if you chose instead to do your own thing and let them do their own thing. There are times when that might be the case (like when I'm trying to make dinner and need them to watch a show for half an hour so I can finish), but even in those situations, be sure to ask them questions about what they watched and maybe even what they learned from the show or movie. That constant level of interest and curiosity in their life can only help with those harder conversations that happen later in life when they inevitably make a bad choice or misstep. And think about it—all you have to do is sit and be present.

Take Time to Move

One of the things we stress in our district is the physical, emotional, and mental well-being of our students and adults. Sitting for several hours on end absorbing content is poor both physically and mentally. Couple that sitting with hours of staring at a screen, and you know have poor physical and eye health combined with a lack of oxygen flow to the brain.

A rule of thumb that I try to follow as a teacher of kids and adults is the 20-minute rule. In its purest form, I try and chunk part of the learning into 20-minute segments with little breaks or transitions in between. Dr. Donna Wilson outlines many great strategies that reinforce this technique and many others in her Edutopia article titled "Move Your Body, Grow Your Brain" (mrhook.it/move).

In the article she mentions the need to "chunk" the day into smaller segments and the powerful effects that movement and physical activity have on the brain and learning. According to research, having some 15 to 45 minutes of movement greatly increases learning retention and decreases distraction and off-task behavior (Wilson, 2014). As someone who facilitates all-day work-shops with adults, I see the difference in behavior and attitude following a fun 5-minute brain break. Doing a simple brain break—like those I share in my third book about coaching and professional learning—can really open up the oxygen flow to the brain and cause laughter, which also has positive effects on the brain.

As a parent at home with kids who may be playing a game for several hours or binge-watching their favorite series, it's important to remember these effects of movement on the brain as well as eye fatigue. One way to balance these binge screen sessions is to break them up into smaller parts. After watching a 30-minute show, have your child go outside for 5 or 10 minutes, or maybe complete a quick chore.

Gaming can be a little harder, because there usually aren't natural stopping points. One effective technique I've seen parents use and I've employed myself is using a simple timer to alert the child to take a break. Most games can be paused and then quickly returned to following the break. I've seen firsthand the effects of this break with my middle child, who is a screen addict of sorts. Her behavior and attitude deteriorate the longer she stares at a screen, but forcing her to take little breaks throughout the screen binge seem to balance her attitude. What normally would be a fight to turn off the screen (resulting in long-drawn-out sob sessions) becomes almost instant without complaint when we tie in mini-breaks.

PARENT TOOLKIT

Eye-timers

Purpose: Reduce long screen time or sitting sessions and increase movement.

Apps/tools: Eyetimer app (http://mrhook.it/eye), 30/30 app (http://3030.binary-hammer.com/), timer app on your phone, or egg timer.

Setup: Using an app or timer, work with your child on determining appropriate times to take breaks from screens or other long periods of sitting. At first, the parent may need to monitor and enforce the timer, but ideally the child learns to self-regulate and set the timer themselves.

You know it's a success when: Your child is setting their own (appropriate) limits for screen time and self-regulating their own seat time and movement.

Circadian Rhythms

Russell Foster is a neuroscientist who studies sleep and sleep patterns in adults and young adults. (Watch his full TED talk here: mrhook.it/sleep.) One of the findings in his research is the reduction in sleep that our bodies are experiencing as we advance with technology. Part of the reasoning behind this reduction in sleep and deeper REM sleep is the fact that we are "always on." In some ways, our constant connection to the world and perceived need to be looking at screens until late into the night affects our sleep.

The scientific reason for this is the internal clock, or circadian rhythm, that our bodies set for us. These primitive rhythms are set to alert the brain whenever bright light (like sunlight) is present. When light isn't present, the brain releases endorphins to help guide the body and brain into a deep sleep. Foster suggests that we try to reduce bright lights and screens about 30 minutes before we plan to go to sleep.

In the time before technology, bright lights, and screens, this wasn't an issue. When the sun went down, people went to sleep. They woke up when the sun came up. However, when you introduce bright light (like the one you turn on before brushing your teeth at night) or look at your phone before going to bed, your upset your internal clock. Your brain thinks it is still daylight and actually holds off on releasing the endorphins that help relax your body and control your bladder when you sleep.

As a parent of a child in a mobile device initiative, you might find this news somewhat troubling. "So

PARENT TOOLKIT

Reduce Blue Light

Purpose: By reducing the amount of blue light from screens, the body's circadian rhythms are not as disrupted and regular sleep is more obtainable.

Apps/tools: F.lux for Android, Mac, and PC (justgetflux.com) or the Night Shift setting on iOS 9 or above.

Setup: Using the tools above, set your devices to go into a dimmer/warmer mode of light later in the evening. This can be done with a timer or based on the actual sunrise and sunset times in your area.

You know it's a success when: Your child is sleeping better, which results in better attitude, health, and learning retention during the day.

you mean to tell me my child isn't getting enough sleep because he is up all night doing homework online? Isn't that the school's fault?" In some ways, you would be correct. The fact that much of the learning is now happening online means an increase in screen time for learning. However, when you think about the amount of screen time spent on entertainment and other ventures (more than 6 1/2 hours for teenagers), the use of screens for learning shouldn't be in addition to these times online.

Besides the tools I mention in the parent toolkit, one of the most effective ways to manage sleep and screens is to work with your child on outlining what work they need to do online. If there is a major project that requires quite a bit of internet research, they should try and do that project earlier in the night. Start with the end in mind and determine when it is that you want your child to go to sleep. Let's say it's 9:30 PM. If that's the case and you know you need to dim lights 30 minutes earlier, that gives you from the time you return from school until 9:00 PM to complete your online homework. Once you take time out for dinner (remember, no technology at the table) and any other activities or after-hours sports, you might have 2 or 3 hours at best to complete the work and not have it affect sleep.

All of this may seem like a futile battle when you see the infiltration of screens into your own lives and what it means for sleep. Looking at the chart based on Dr. Foster's research (Figure 5.2), you realize that teenagers need around 9 hours of sleep and the average adult around 8 hours of sleep. Many adults and kids are falling well short of this. That lack of sleep affects behavior, diet, and attention, all of which can affect learning and retention in school.

Although there will be days when you and your child will not meet your required hours of sleep, we should be striving to balance sleep time with awake time in our lives. One of the ways to help with this is reducing the amount of blue light our eyes capture (most common in florescent lights and digital screens). While having warmer and softer light is still not as effective as no light at all, it does allow for the brain to begin the sleep process and endorphin release sooner. As you can see in the Parent Toolkit in this chapter, technology companies are beginning to be aware of this and are releasing tools that help transition from blue light to warm light later in the evening.

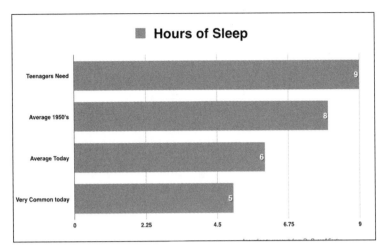

Figure 5.2 Average night sleep chart

As parents in the modern world, we are all vying with our kids' screens for their attention. There are a lot of positive aspects to our students being connected and having access to information at the touch of a finger. However, as with everything in life, balance is the key. Although each and every child is different, we should always work with our children on setting limits, monitoring their screen time, and making adjustments to their nightly routine to ensure that they get a quality night's sleep to help them learn and grow for the days and years to come.

CHAPTER 6

SOCIAL MEDIA

According to recent (2015) Pew Internet research, kids are online all the time (mrhook.it/pew). They are posting pictures, playing games, communicating with each other, and watching videos. Most kids don't rest in one single place for too long, either, when it comes to social media. In fact, more than 71% of kids visit multiple social media sites daily.

So why are they going online, and what are they doing when they get there? When I asked high school students in my district and in other districts, their answers varied but generally fell into these four main categories:

"To connect with friends"

"To get the news"

"To see what's happening with my family and friends"

"To be social"

These answers make sense. However, a parent who doesn't understand social media, and its impact on our society, may think of social media like this:

"A place to cyberbully"

"A place to post inappropriate images or words"

"A place to waste your time"

Indeed, when I asked teens if their parents understood their use of social media, the answers varied. Some said their parents not only "got" social media, but that they were on it more often than the kids (more on that in a moment). The students who said that their parents don't understand it often claimed that parents would take a single negative news item or story and, based on that, condemn all forms of online communication.

The truth, as usual, lies somewhere in between adults' understanding and use of social media and its use and understanding by our kids. Social media really took off after the creation of Facebook in 2004, coupled with the creation of the smartphone a few years later. We now all have an avenue to post and share whatever we want, from wherever we want.

As with anything new in technology, in the early days of social media, some people used it as an avenue to post inappropriate comments and pornography, and as a means to bully others anonymously. Although these traits still exist in modern uses of social media, as teens and adults become more savvy with its use as a communication and connection tool, as well as understanding its possible effects on future job searches or college recruitment, self-regulation is on the rise. The time when it was still possible to give the excuse, "Oh, I didn't know everyone could see that" is quickly coming to an end, and as millennials become bosses in the workplace, they will no longer accept an excuse like "I made a mistake when I was younger and posted that inappropriate comment online."

"Sharenting"

A quick side note here to once again reiterate the importance of modeling from adults. One way that we should try to help our kids is by not oversharing their lives online. The phrase "sharenting" was invented by people tired of seeing every accomplishment of a young child growing up. Some parents (and I've been guilty of this at times) want to let the world know when little Jimmy has lost each and every tooth and that magical moment when he goes potty by himself. Although these are prideful moments for parents, there are some things better left unshared.

Digital Permanence

Nothing is truly ever anonymous or temporary online.

If you get nothing else out of this book or chapter, remember that phrase and share it regularly with your friends, family, and kids. The internet catalogs everything, and even if you think it's gone, it's not. One great example of this is an activity I did with my teenage niece, Jordan. She was getting heavily into Snapchat, which is a social media platform that lets you post funny photos or videos that soon disappear.

Jordan showed me some of the funny faces she was posting and gave me the backstory of the app and why her friends used it. When I asked her if they ever posted inappropriate stuff, she hesitated. I then relayed a story with her about how a man in 2014 was able to quickly hack the Snapchat server and access all the user accounts, including their photos. Her face began to turn pale. I then showed her how I could use the internet WayBack Machine (archive. org) to accomplish the same task. Now she began to squirm. This was a great message and realization to share with her—that even if she thought the photos were disappearing from the phones, they still were stored somewhere on the internet.

What Is Social Media?

It's interesting what we think of when the words "social media" are mentioned. Parents', minds tend to drift to a couple of different places—mainly Facebook and bad things with teens. For kids, it's actually a very different experience.

Looking at the definitions of the terms "social" and "media" (courtesy of Merriam-Webster), the technical definition of social media is

> Spending time together interacting and communicating [the social part] through a system which can be spread to a large number of people [the media part].

As I've mentioned, one of the lucky aspects of my job is that I get to spend time talking with kids from all over the world. Given this dedicated time with students who live and breathe in this world, I like to make the most of it. Rather than turn this time into a lecture about the good and bad about social media, I like to gamify it—not only to increase their level of involvement, but also to help keep me current with the things they are into and the reasons why they trend toward certain sites.

Is Everything Social Media?

One of my favorite challenges when working with a group of teens is to separate them into teams of three or four, then give them 2 minutes and challenge them to name as many social media platforms as they can. Although I know this will bring about some silly answers, I also know that competitiveness will kick in at some point. Many of the teams have had more than 25 different responses, including 32 from one team of middle school students. I did my best to collect these quickly and have students explain the ones I didn't get.

Here are a couple of the lists from some groups I worked with (Figure 6.1). Excuse the bad handwriting, as I was trying to capture these quickly.

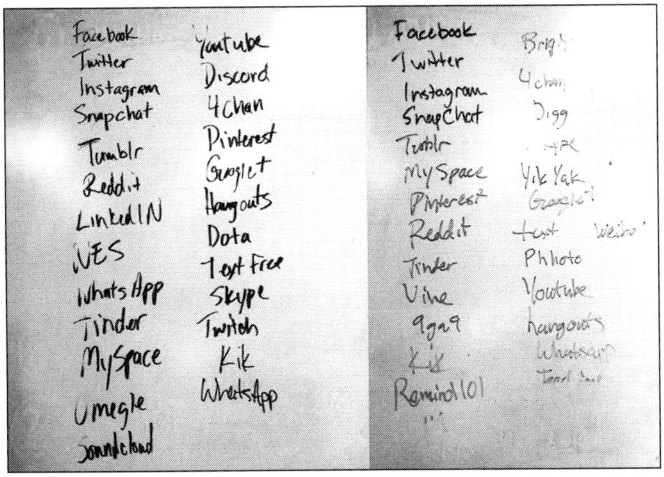

Figure 6.1 A brainstormed list of social media sites in a 2-minute challenge with teens.

A few things stand out when I look through these lists. First, there are what we would consider "typical" social media sites listed by the kids. Facebook, Twitter, Instagram, Snapchat, and Tumblr seem to be the most popular and most mentioned. Another thing that really stood out was the sheer number of apps and websites they mentioned as social media sites. They varied from dating sites like Tinder to video service sites like YouTube or Vimeo.

Then things got interesting.

One of the students stood up and said "Amazon." I went to write it down and paused. … "You mean, like the place you go to buy stuff?"

Yes. The student began to explain his thinking. He says that if you review something, you can actually use that space to interact with customers and companies, therefore making it "social" in nature. Looking at our definition of social media stated earlier, I would say he's actually onto something here. At that point students began to mention many other platforms and places where they are social online.

This left me somewhat floored. Not only were these lists growing, but now everything could be social media.

Agree/Disagree Challenge

Another activity I like to try with students is the agree/disagree challenge. I ask students to either stand up or sit down based on a topic or statement I post on the board. If they agree with the statement, they stand up. If they disagree, they sit down. Here are some of my common questions/statements and some of the results based on live case studies (percentages based on approximate estimates of the number of kids standing or sitting):

Statement 1: Cyberbullying is getting worse.

Agree: 65%

Disagree: 35%

Responses: Many of the students agreed with the statement with the rationale that because there are so many more social media sites out there, there must be more cyberbullying. Some students mentioned the ease with which you could be anonymous now on many of these platforms, which makes it easier to cyberbully. Those who disagreed said that they felt their generation is much more aware of the permanence of their actions online and how everything has a trace, even if you think it's anonymous. According to an article by *U.S. News & World Report,* it's actually been on a steady decline since 2005 (read the article here: mrhook.it/bully).

Statement 2: You can post a photo, then delete it and it will be gone forever.

Agree: 0%

Disagree: 100%

Apparently students across the United States have heard this loud and clear. Not a single student even stood up as a joke. They know that if it's online, it could be accessed. However, when I relayed the story about my niece Jordan I mentioned earlier, it made some of them squirm in their seats. So although they believe this statement, their actions may not necessarily follow suit when it comes to posting "temporary" photos.

Statement 3: Adults don't understand what teens do on social media.

Agree: 50%

Disagree: 50%

This one and the next statement divided the groups the most. Those who agreed with the statement mentioned in some cases that parents hear a negative story about an app or a kid on social media and assume that means that only terrible things are happening online. Another mentioned that his parents just don't take the time to ask and understand what an app is and how he is using it. One student summed it up by saying, "Imagine if *their* parents told them to stay off the phone because someone could potentially prank call them. That's how we feel sometimes when it comes to social media and our parents." Those who disagreed argued that parents are much more tech-savvy these days. They have smartphones, easy access to other parents (via social media, ironically), and can Google search just about anything.

Statement 4: I think my social media use could help me get into college or land my first job.

Agree: 50%

Disagree: 50%

Another statement that had the groups split right down the middle. In fact, it was almost a corollary with the previous statement in terms of who agreed and who disagreed. Those who disagreed claimed that it depended on the type of job, which might make this statement false. They also said that they had been made so scared to get on social media that they hoped it didn't hurt them in the future. Many of the students who agreed mentioned how it could help build their online profile and make connections that would help in the future.

One precocious 12-year-old girl said, "More and more colleges and businesses are looking at your online profile everyday. That means there is a great opportunity to use that profile to help you land a job or get into college." We'll dive deeper into this subject in the final chapter, but I think it's always one that you and your child should have in the back of your minds.

Communication between Home and School about Social Media

I often say the lines between home and school have been permanently blurred. As soon as schoolwork becomes digital or a district adopts a mobile learning initiative, there is crossover between the actions of the students at home and at school. For this last section in this chapter, I'm going to share with you two actual letters that went home to parents in our district relating to social media concerns and issues. I share these with you as a parent to help keep you informed, but also to open up a dialogue between families and schools. If you are an administrator or teacher reading this book, feel free to steal any parts of what follows in an effort to better communicate with your community.

Date: February 10, 2015

Dear Eanes ISD Parents,

This past week we discovered a new trend among teens with their personal use of technology. While seemingly innocent on the surface, the latest in hidden photo-sharing apps could potentially cause trouble with our youth down the road, especially in the area of "sexting." While the Eanes ISD staff have taken the necessary precautions to block/restrict these types of apps on our network and devices, students still can engage in misbehavior on their own personal devices, which can lead to serious distraction and, even more seriously, possible prosecution.

Similar to last semester's issues with the Yik Yak app, we are once again asking for parents to keep an eye out for the following apps (or similar ones) that might be making the rounds on your child's phone.

We are sharing these tools and resources with parents in order to promote discussion around responsible decision making, to correct poor choices, and to open up a dialogue between parent and teen about their digital lives. What follows is information about some specific hidden photo-sharing apps, next steps to take, and where to go for help and support as a parent.

Keep Safe Private Photo Vault is one of many new "secret vault" type apps making their way through the app stores of Apple and Android. This app is advertised as a way to keep photos and videos safe behind a private PIN and not post them on your public photo roll.

The app is easy enough to identify. However, if you share iCloud accounts or check your child's photo roll regularly, you won't notice it, as photos don't appear there. While hiding photos is one issue, our concern is with the "Invite friends" premium feature. With this enabled, kids can potentially share photos privately without anyone knowing. One additional premium feature is called "Secret Door." This allows you to make the app look like another app. Pressing and holding down on the "fake" app enables the PIN pad.

Next steps

If your child is a Keep Safe Private Photo Vault user (or a user of another "private vault" type app), a conversation should happen with him/her about why they feel the need to hide their photos and share them privately. If you don't see the app, but suspect it may have been downloaded, you can also check in the Updates section of the App Store under "Purchased" on your child's phone. Any apps ever downloaded are stored there.

Additionally, there are new apps that are disguised as a calculator or a folder on the device, making them harder to find. Two such apps include Fake Calculator and Best Secret Folder. (Figure 6.2)

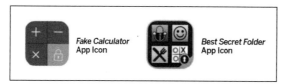

Figure 6.2 Secret photo sharing app icons.

These apps look innocent, and most of the calculator apps actually are real WORKING calculators. However, if you punch in a secret combination of numbers and symbols, you can "unlock" the secret photo compartment hidden behind the calculator.

Rather than checking every single app on your child's device, one quick way to check on an iOS device is to go to Settings->Privacy->Camera. There is a list of every app that uses or has used the camera at one time or another. (Figure 6.3)

While deleting the app takes care of the immediate issue, there may be a larger issue at hand when it comes to the use of private photo sharing by your child. Please take this opportunity to have that conversation about how NOTHING on the internet is truly anonymous or temporary.

So ... Why should I worry about this?

Much like with Yik Yak in the fall, it is likely that many students will learn about these apps from friends and be curious to try them. Teens have a certain level of curiosity and experimentation anyway, but with the added peer pressure, it could lead to a more serious issue like "sexting." Texas Attorney General Ken Paxton goes into the details of sexting laws in the state on this site (http://mrhook.it/laws). While the majority of these cases are tied to state courts, here is some more information on the federal side of things (http://mrhook.it/fedlaw).

What else is out there?

Besides those mentioned above, there are many other apps being made that provide the same service. Here is a Mashable.com post (http://mrhook.it/sextapps) that describes seven different apps for iOS and Android that hide photos and videos. Much like social media and kids, the best method of avoiding any type of negative behavior with this technology is openness, awareness, and communication with your child.

Figure 6.3 Seeing what apps are accessing your camera.

Where can I get help and support?

Common Sense Media (http://commonsense.org) always has helpful resources for parents and kids. Here is an article for parents on how to discuss sexting with your teen (http://mrhook.it/sexttalk).

Thank you for taking the time to not only review all this information but also to talk with your child. We know that it may be difficult, but it is important to have an ongoing conversation about social media and digital footprints. If you have any other questions or concerns, please contact either your campus administrators, counselors, or me.

It takes a village to raise a child. The more we communicate, the better the learning experience for our kids.

Date: January 11, 2016

Parents of Secondary Students,

Adolescents today have access to knowledge and learning right at their fingertips. They are accessing and creating content on their school-issued iPads and on school computers. More and more of our students also have their own smartphones to access the web and social media. With that access comes greater responsibility and education about the appropriate use of technology and social media. This letter is intended to help raise awareness with families about some trends around the country and possibly among our own students.

Sexting

There have been several recent instances at high schools around the country of teenagers transmitting illicit images of themselves to other students (also known as "sexting"). There was a recent case at a Colorado High School.

In the case of the school in Colorado, many students used a photo vault app like the one we shared last year that looks like a calculator. Students exchange these photos like trading cards, and in some cases, students feel pressured to share inappropriate photos with other students. Once these photos are shared, they can be shared with others and even posted on the web.

Cyberbullying via apps like Brighten and After School

Bullying is not a new occurrence in schools, unfortunately. With technology and social media, there are now new venues for this same bad behavior. Two particular apps that have been brought to our attention as pathways for cyberbullying are the Brighten app and the After School app. Brighten was originally intended as a way for people to send random compliments to each other to "brighten" their day; however, students have used this platform to anonymously bully, make racial slurs, and post other inappropriate comments about other students. Brighten has a way to issue a "time out" if inappropriate behavior is pointed out, but they are not actively monitoring posts. When I reached out to them, they responded with this: "If you are seeing specific instances of bullying, please send people to alec@brighten.in and I can personally take care of it."

The After School app is promoted as a way to anonymously post messages about your school or those in your school. According to After School data, currently 363 Westlake students are listed as users of this app. When I reached out to them, they responded with the following: "We are very, very sorry about the experience some of your students are having on After School. Our moderators and I are keeping an extra close eye on Eanes Independent School District. We added extra moderators. We are launching an investigation." They also shared this link: 5 Tips for Parents on Monitoring Their Child's Social Media Use (http://mrhook. it/5tips), which contains some good nuggets of information.

Why are you telling me about this?

We are sharing this news with you both to raise awareness and also to encourage you to have conversations with your child about these apps and sexting. While we can monitor school-issued devices, we can not directly monitor what students are doing on their personal devices. However, if we suspect a student is doing something inappropriate with their personal device, we will confiscate the item and contact parents.

What do I do if my child receives an inappropriate photo or is cyberbullied?

Many students are afraid to turn in other students or afraid that they themselves will get in trouble when it comes to having sexting-like messages on their personal devices. Some students actually feel pressured to take illicit images of themselves as a form of cyberbullying. If a student receives an image and reports it immediately, there will be no punishment as the infraction is being reported. However, if there is intent to possess or promote inappropriate or illicit images, there will be disciplinary action.

What does the law say about this in regard to sexting?

While there are some differences in terms of age (18 years old being the line between minor and adult), the possession or promotion of illicit content of a minor via sexting is similar to being in possession or promotion of child pornography. According to Texas SB 407—(http://mrhook.it/sb407) A student in "possession" (having illicit content for an unreasonable amount of time) or "promoting" (sending/sharing illicit content with others) can be charged with anything from a Class C misdemeanor to a second degree felony.

What is the district doing to help with this?

Our counselors and administration are aware of the situation and ready to help any students that come forward with information around this topic. In addition, we are holding "social media talks" with student groups at the high school as well as discussing digital citizenship and online safety at all levels. For parents, we will continue to host parent talks during booster club meetings and also send out information on our Digital Parent Newsletter (you can sign up here: http://mrhook.it/news). Starting in the spring, we will hold our 4th "Digital Parenting" course (for more information go to http://eanesisd.net/leap/parents). We have formally requested, as we did with Yik Yak last year, that the app developers put up a "geofence" around our schools. A geofence would block use of the app even on personal phones. However, these companies are not required to comply with this request, and even if they do, the geofence is only active around the school, not at home.

What can I do as a parent?

Again, we think it's important that you have repeated critical conversations with your child about their use of personal technology. Talk to them about the risks of inappropriate use when it comes to sexting and cyberbullying, including breaking the law. Also, most smartphones have ways of checking which apps are being used. For instance, on an iPhone, owned by over 70% of our students, there is a way to check battery usage in settings (with iOS9). Through this check, you can see what apps your child has accessed in the last 24 hours and last 7 days. (see figure 6.4)

Figure 6.4 Battery usage check on iOS

Please report any situations that you are aware of to either the local authorities or school administration. We want to make sure our students know that we are having common conversations between home and school when it comes to sexting and cyberbullying.

Thank you for your support, and please let us know if you have any questions or concerns.

Again, I share these letters not to make you worried or fearful as a parent, but rather, to encourage you to communicate with other parents and, most importantly, with your kids. Although they may have greater knowledge of the social media tools out there, your wisdom and years of experience is something they cannot suppress with the click of a button. Keep communicating, keep discussing, and always remember—nothing is temporary or anonymous online.

PARENT TOOLKIT

Google Yourself

Purpose: Determine what your online reputation looks like when you search yourself.

Apps/tools: Google search engine

Set-up: Launch google.com and make sure you are not logged into your Google account as this will affect the results that are presented. Then, type in your name in quotations marks (i.e. "John Smith") to see what kind of results are revealed.

You know it's a success when: Your child recognizes that things they post or things their friends post affects their online image. Rather than avoiding online interactions, they can choose to control their online reputation by posting positive messages and sharing resources with the masses.

CHAPTER 7

HOUSEHOLD GUIDELINES

"I'm just sick and tired of fighting with my kids and their technology."

This is a statement I have heard over and over throughout my years of facilitating parent workshops and discussions. There is this feeling in many households that there needs to be a "fight" or "battle" when it comes to kids and technology. This battle can happen in other arenas, too (in my household, getting kids to bed on time), but generally technology seems to be viewed in this light—partly because it's new, and partly because we as parents don't quite understand the use or entertainment value of the devices or social media sites.

A big reason to put some sort of shared guidelines in place sooner rather than later is that they help avoid those battles. Without agreed-upon guidelines and rules, you might find yourself in the following scenario.

Over-gaming Scenario

Your son is playing his video game and not doing his homework or chores. You try and approach it calmly at first and say, "Hey, son, I know you are having fun playing that game, but could you wrap it up and finish your homework and chores first?"

By asking it like a question, you empower him to respond with a yes or no and give him some level of control of the situation. However, you also run the risk of him saying "just a minute," and then continuing to play for hours.

A more strict (and even less effective way) would be to say, "Hey listen, I don't understand why you keep goofing around with that silly game. You *know* you have work to do, yet you make the poor choice of playing that game instead. Stop procrastinating and turn that thing off before I throw it out the window!"

In the above scenario and final response, you have effectively thrown in judgment and a fake consequence to solve a problem. You may think the game he is playing is silly, but he obviously feels it warrants his attention much more than homework and chores. Also, saying you'll throw his device out the window relays your anger, but again, it's something you are unlikely to do (hopefully).

One of the things I've stressed over and over in this book is the need to have constant communication with your child about their activity on their devices. In the next two chapters, we'll go into some rules and also restrictions that you can put in place to help curb their inappropriate use. Please know that no set of rules or restrictions can replace honest discussion and conversation with your child. I'll also throw in some more scenarios like the one above and give some options for responses. Please know that every situation and every child is different, so the scenarios and guidelines I offer are suggestions and not hard-and-fast rules to follow.

The 24-Hour Rule

Before we discuss some guidelines and ideas for creating them, I want to mention an idea that a few parents I've been working with recently have deployed in their house with some success. It is actually a process very similar to what the Federal Aviation Administration (FAA) puts in place for their air traffic controllers. Whenever a mistake is made or a potential mishap is avoided, the FAA puts in place a 24-hour rule of protection for the person making the mistake. What this means is that if someone makes a mistake but then reports it within 24 hours, they will be free of traditional punishment. The rationale behind this rule is that if people share and learn from the mistake, it will make all other air traffic controllers more aware and responsive, potentially avoiding major disasters down the road.

In the case of our kids, we can deploy a similar rule. Kids will make mistakes in life whether it be virtual or real. We want them to learn from their mistakes but can't help them if they hide them from us. Having a rule of 24-hour protection to report an inappropriate finding or action encourages our kids to talk to us about things they come across and also learn from their mistakes before making potentially greater mistakes down the road. Here's a scenario:

Stumbling across Inappropriate Material Scenario

While doing research for a project on rainforests, your 10-year-old does an image search for "rain" which inexplicably brings up images of a partially nude night club dancer who goes by the same name.

Without the 24-hour rule:

Your child is somewhat curious about the photos but also knows they shouldn't be looking at them. Rather than tell you, they continue to look through the web and click on links that turn out to be spam. A few days later, their computer becomes infected, at which point they confess to what they were doing and hand you a hefty computer repair bill.

With the 24-hour rule:

Your child is somewhat curious about the photos but also knows he/she shouldn't be looking at them. They know they are inappropriate and also know you have a 24-hour rule about mistakes being made on the internet or in real life. He/she brings it to your attention, at which point you can have a discussion about what they saw and also talk about "phishing" sites and how viruses/spam can come from such places. The computer isn't affected, and you figure out how to put on a stronger image filter to avoid future missteps.

This scenario is tricky because some of the damage has already been done by the child seeing the inappropriate image. Much like the case of the FAA, at that point you are in damage control and adjustment mode. However, if your child doesn't tell you, under the protection of the 24-hour rule, the range of possible outcomes continue to get worse. If your child reveals what was discovered immediately, you can have an on-point (albeit somewhat uncomfortable) conversation about what your child saw and also make necessary adjustments to filters and image searches to avoid it happening again in the future.

The 24-hour rule is a great general rule to put in place in a household—but know there might be the occasion when it has to be broken, especially if a child or teen starts to abuse it. Knowing there is freedom from consequence could cause them to test their limits more often and then tell you about it after the fact. The basis for the 24-hour rule is that there are consequences for every action, but the severity of those consequences is made greater by your child keeping it from you.

Purpose of Household Guidelines

Regardless of what rules and guidelines you decide to put into action in your household about technology, devices, and social media, you should always evaluate those rules as an opportunity for growth more than punishment. Just like the 24-hour rule, this can often lead to some difficult conversations—but remember that a hard conversation now can help your child make a better decision later in life.

One of the other purposes of household guidelines is to strive to have your kids self-regulate and monitor their actions online. You shouldn't feel like a hawk constantly circling around your child when they go online or chat with someone via social media. While you should still be aware of what they are doing in general, you need to also encourage them to make the right choices. Once they leave your house after high school, they will have to make those choices completely on their own at that point. If you hand-hold them for too long throughout their teen years, they won't be accustomed to self-regulating bad behavior or making correct choices on their own.

Shared Ownership and Scenarios

When you set out to create rules of the household (whether it be for technology or not), you want to include your kids in this process. If they have some early say in the brainstorming phase of rule creation, they will be more likely to follow the rules and adhere to the consequences of breaking them. This brainstorm process can also be a covert opportunity to discuss the rationale behind certain social media tools or the actions of your child (and his/her friends) online.

In collaborating with your child, be thinking and discussing possible scenarios that they might encounter and how they would handle these. Going through scenarios can help unearth some ideas about rules and consequences for negative behavior or breaking the rules.

Here are a few scenarios to think about with your kids and some possible ideas for rules or guidelines about the behavior.

Screen Time Binge Scenario

Your child is going on a marathon of television watching, YouTube viewing, or gaming. You know that this isn't good for their brain, eyes, or health, so you try to intervene.

Without household guidelines solution:

You can either let them continue on the binge and suffer the guilt of letting them do it, or you can make them stop. Making them stop involves the potential of a meltdown and also a fight or argument, as they don't understand why you are doing this to them.

With household guidelines solution:

Knowing that screen time can be an issue, you and your child create a rule where every 30 minutes they have to take a 5-minute break. They are also not to go over 2 hours of viewing in a day without a significant break or other activity.

By creating the rules ahead of time with your child, you have set in place some agreed-upon terms. Additionally, you could add in some consequences if they choose to break the rules and continue the inappropriate action. Just like the creation of the rules, the consequences should be decided on together. You'll find that often your child may come up with harsher consequences than you! In the screen-time scenario, a consequence might be the loss of "entertainment-based" screen time in the next 24 or 48 hours. Having the mutually created rule in place helps avoid potential clashes and arguments and helps your child self-regulate their screen time more effectively.

Drama has always been a part of growing up, especially in middle school. Technology has amplified the ease with which drama can grow and has taken away an emotional and empathetic element of it, as people are now just words and emojis. These are extremely hard for your kids to avoid once they own a device. It might be Snapchats or texts or tweets—regardless, there are times when they will get pulled into these conversations and not even know it. There are other times when they might instigate it.

While having a general rule or guideline about this behavior is advisable, this is one case where the action isn't quite so black and white. Rather, this is an opportunity to have a discussion and lend some guidance to your child about how they should respond and gracefully exit a drama session over text messages. The good news is, by putting some household guidelines in place, that discussion can take place well before anything like this actually happens and when less emotion is involved, as that can cloud judgment and increase frustration.

Guidelines like "no texting at the dinner table" and "treat others with kindness and empathy" can help steer your child in the right direction. In our house we have a simple rule—"If you don't have something nice to say, say nothing at all."

Group Texting Drama Scenario

Your middle school daughter is a part of multiple texting chains with friends. This starts after school ends and carries through dinnertime. These aren't school-related texts and are actually all about creating drama with other friends.

Without household guidelines solution:

You tell her to get off the phone, especially at dinner. A struggle ensues, at which point you take the phone away and say she can get it back in the morning. This causes additional drama, as she now feels left out of the conversation with her friends.

With household guidelines solution:

Working with your daughter ahead of time, you've discussed when it's appropriate to text with friends and what the content should be about. In this scenario, both time and content are inappropriate, and she already knows that those are important in the rules you created. She tells her friends she's off to have family time and tries to steer them into a more positive direction away from the drama.

The Reality TV Star Scenario

Your teenage son has decided that he wants to be the next reality TV star, so he creates his own YouTube channel that involves him blowing things up in creative ways. He makes videos regularly and posts them almost daily. In the comment threads, people suggest he blow up his mom's car, which he considers.

Without household guidelines solution:

You know he enjoys blowing things up but are concerned about his health and the amount of destruction he's causing. Add to that the social media layer and the fact that his "Blow Up Boy" channel is now popular, and you face an almost insurmountable scenario. Ultimately, you tell him to remove the channel and to stop blowing things up, which cause him to have a fit of rage about the fact you've taken away his creative outlet.

With household guidelines solution:

There's a rule in place about being respectful of your own and others' personal property. Knowing this and your son's need to be hands-on and share, you encourage your son to create a Do-It-Yourself channel where he takes common items and "remixes" them into something cool and useful. His "DIY Boy" channel takes off. Your agreed-upon rule about "oversharing" also kicks in here, and he decides to post a show weekly that is well-produced and planned.

This is obviously an extreme scenario, but one thing I'll mention now is that all the scenarios I've listed in this chapter are loosely based on things I've actually encountered. Compared to our childhood, kids today can easily be published and viewable to the entire world via a blog, YouTube channel, or other means. Having a voice and confidence in their work can be a powerful learning mechanism if done for good rather than destruction, as in this scenario. What might start out as a cute kid blowing up stuffed animals with firecrackers can quickly go downhill. Aided with an online audience, it almost becomes addicting to the child as well, which creates another set of challenges to overcome as a parent trying to steer him in a more positive direction.

This scenario also highlights the fact that whatever rules or guidelines you put in place, they shouldn't be stagnant. If you created household guidelines before little Johnny became obsessed with explosives, then you should add or amend the guidelines when you notice this becoming a problem so he has some say in what is right and what is wrong.

Again, I cannot stress enough the importance in creating these guidelines ahead of time and also inviting your child to help you create them. With his input, you might decide that some rules like "Thou shalt not destroy property" need to exist. You might also decide that rules like "We only post positive messages/videos online" or "We will not overshare online" need to be put in place as well for the family.

Texting Immediacy Scenario

Your 11-year-old daughter has just gotten her first cell phone and is respectful of the texting rules of the house. She doesn't text all day and night, nor does she start drama. However, she's run into a problem where she expects immediate feedback from friends when she sends them a text. She sends one friend a message and when she doesn't get a response, she sends several other messages over an hour's time and eventually starts to cry because she thinks her friend is ignoring her.

Without household guidelines solution:

This baffles you as a parent, and you aren't quite sure if there is a problem with the friend or not. You tell your daughter to be patient, but she's already beside herself. You end up calling the parent of the other child, only to learn that they have a "no texting during homework or dinner" rule in their house, which is why she wasn't responding.

With household guidelines solution:

Teaching empathy can be a hard thing for teens or tweens. They sometimes get so wrapped up in themselves that they can't imagine what the person on the other end of the line is doing. Knowing this, you work with your daughter ahead of time and create a guideline before she gets her cell phone: She needs to not only be respectful of her friends' rules, but also empathetic to their actions and not jump to conclusions.

This is a scenario that a close friend of mine stumbled on. It wasn't something she had considered, but in a world where immediacy of communication seems to be commonplace, there are emotional repercussions to not getting immediate feedback. When our kids are young, we stress the importance of others' personal physical space. We also need to know be cognizant of their personal virtual space and have a sense of awareness that not all kids follow the same rules or have the same access as others.

Keeping the Guidelines Positive

I could write an entire book based solely on scenarios. I mentioned a few here to get your mind thinking about things you might encounter or may have already encountered. After you've discussed the scenarios with your kids and brainstormed ideas around how to handle specific situations, you should then work on making a set of actual guidelines.

For the sake of your sanity and also to make these rules easier to follow, I would suggest limiting the household rules to no more than 10, and if possible, try to whittle it down to 4 to 6 rules. One way to do this is by grouping some rules into a general rule or guideline. Having two rules that say "No screen time after 9 p.m." and "Limit binge watching to no more than 2 hours with breaks" can be combined into a single rule that states, "Be aware of screen time and its effect on my mental and physical health."

Keeping the rule more general doesn't take away from the discussion or brainstorming of scenarios behind it. Also, giving it a more positive spin rather than saying "Limit your screen time" makes it more impactful and easier to adhere to. A child choosing to break that rule does so knowing that it's affecting their brain and decreasing physical movement because it's stated in the rule.

Some other good ones I've seen used include:

"Technology and online behavior are always out in the open." (helps to keep devices out of from behind closed doors and also opens up what they are posting online)

"I'm respectful of others' time and traditions." (helps with empathy about restrictions others may have and also not texting/calling at all hours of the night)

"Be kind to others." (helps with both online and real-life behaviors)

"Be positive with my words and actions" (keeps drama to a minimum as well as potential bullying or shaming online)

"Be honest, open and own my mistakes." (encourages them to take risks, but also to engage in conversation when a mistake happens)

Signing on the Dotted Line

There are thousands of these kinds of rules available on Pinterest or through web searches. However, I'd caution you against taking that clever teakwood sign with chalk and posting it as a work of art. These guidelines should be malleable and amendable in the future. Also, they are to be created and agreed to by *everyone* in the family. So, when you make the poster, have everyone sign on the bottom line like a contract. You can refer to this signature in the future should a rule ever be tested or challenged—because it will be.

PARENT TOOLKIT

Creating a Household Guidelines Agreement Poster

Purpose: Hang a poster with agreed-upon household guidelines for technology and life behavior

Apps/tools: Poster paper, chalkboard, or whiteboard

Setup: Go through some scenarios with your kids and brainstorm ideas for rules and consequences. Group these rules into a more general set of guidelines with a positive spin and write them on the poster. Have everyone in the household sign the bottom.

You know it's a success when: Your family avoids potential pitfalls of negative online and social behavior. You find yourself arguing and battling with your kids less and less about their actions with devices, technology, and social media. Your whole family grows closer, communicates more, and learns from each other's mistakes.

CHAPTER 8

TOOLS FOR PARENTS

A lthough I've interspersed many different ideas throughout the book and in the "Parent Toolkit" sections, I know that parents also want other tools and hardware at times to help them monitor their kids and keep them safe. I purposely saved this chapter for much later in the book because I believe the best tool for parents in combating inappropriate use of technology or online behavior is their presence and communication. However, it's also useful to have some tools in place not only to help protect your child from encountering inappropriate content, but also to monitor their actions online.

As with any technology tool, these are constantly being updated, changed, or rendered obsolete. One rule of thumb that I preached early on in my career was having a strong filter on a family computer that was placed somewhere in the center of the house. Now with mobile devices and 4G internet, there are times where no internet filter is being accessed and the "computer" can go anywhere.

Thus, while some of the restrictions and filters in this chapter are specific to a tool or device, be aware that they are ever-changing. Also, as the tools for restriction change, so do the tools for getting around the restriction—which is why we spent several chapters going over scenarios and the hard conversations that need to take place with you and your child.

Caution: These tools *do not* replace parenting.

Tools for iOS Users

Being the director of a 1:1 iPad implementation, I have a heightened sense of awareness when it comes to all things iOS. That coupled with the fact that of the kids in our community who own a phone, 80% have one from Apple. The tools and restrictions mentioned in this section are based on the most up-to-date (summer 2016 as of this writing) tools in the current operating system. As those will change over time, I'll also include some links to resources and places to go to find more information in these areas.

App Management Strategies

One of the biggest concerns we discovered early on was that some students spent a great deal of their screen time on non-instructional or entertainment-based apps. Although we could restrict certain categories, it becomes an almost futile effort to block everything that a child may or may not download. Some of these strategies are iOS-specific, but many of them also exist in some form on other mobile-device operating systems.

In-App Purchases and Credit Card

There's nothing more distressing as a parent than to receive a $200 iTunes bill because your child has downloaded hundreds of different cake toppings for her virtual Hello Kitty cake at 99 cents each. (Hand raised here as a parent who has experienced this exact scenario.) There are two things you need to know about your child's iTunes account: You can (and should) manage the account, and you shouldn't tie a credit card to it. This can be done by "purchasing" a free app when you first create the account and choosing "none" as payment type.

If your child wants to purchase an app or song, you can have them load in credit via iTunes gift cards so they have a set amount that they can manage. If for some reason you do decide to tie a credit card to the account, I'd highly recommend going into restrictions (mentioned below) and turning off the "In-App Purchases" option. This will help you avoid any surprise $200 Hello Kitty cake bills in the future.

Age-Level Restrictions

The Apple iOS operating system comes equipped with a powerful built-in restriction option. This option, when enabled, allows you to control whatever content is coming into the phone regardless of internet filter (Figure 8.1). One word of advice here is that when establishing a restriction passcode, make sure it is one that your kids

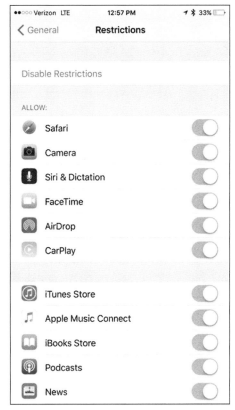

Figure 8.1 Some of the items you can turn off on your phone.

will not know, and also realize that this code is different from the passcode lock of the phone itself.

Going into the general settings and enabling restrictions presents you with many options. You can choose whether or not you want your child to have access to the iTunes store or music. You can turn off the ability to get on the internet at all (Safari) and investigate different restriction options for content. The restrictions for allowed content (Figure 8.2) can be as conservative or open as you feel your child is able to manage.

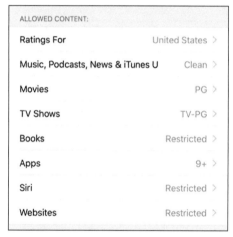

Figure 8.2 Some examples of restrictions place on a student's device.

In our mobile device program, we limit access to many sites early on in a child's educational career, but then slowly open up and allow more content as a child matures. The goal is to have them prepared for the adult world when they leave both our doors and yours. Keeping heavy restrictions on them until they are 18 years old can actually inhibit the development of their own self-control and self-regulation.

There are times when you or your child find an app that might be appropriate, but it carries a higher age restriction for whatever reason. Apps with built-in web browsers (other than Safari) generally always carry with them a 17+ age restriction because the built-in web browser on an app isn't filtered like the Safari app. Also, apps like Facebook carry a 4+ age rating, but to hold a social media account, the user must be 13+ in most cases. So they can download the app, but can't (and really shouldn't) use it until they are of proper age.

App Self-Regulation

Even with these restrictions in place, a child could still download thousands of apps onto their device. Some parents I've worked with have put a rule in place where a child can only have a set number of non-instructional apps on their device. Since these devices are used for learning but also entertainment, kids should be striving for a balance between the two worlds.

If you feel like your child needs heavier monitoring on this front, you could turn off the ability to purchase and/or download apps in the restrictions settings. This means any time that a child needs an app, they have to ask you for permission and the restrictions passcode.

As that method is time consuming, it does give you some semblance of control. A more effective option I have discovered is that instead of turning off the ability to download apps, you turn off the ability to delete them. This would be helpful if you want them to have the ability to download whatever apps they choose, but also want to see what they've downloaded. It also reduces the amount of time they spend asking you to download apps for them, and increases their awareness of how many apps and what kinds of apps they have on their phone, as they can never delete them.

It also says you trust them to make the right choices, but lets them know that if they mess up, they can't hide it.

Website Restrictions

All iOS devices come with a built-in tool to filter web traffic and content. Making adjustments to this restriction only affect web traffic on the Safari app, so if your child has a different browser such as Chrome or Opera, they can still get around the filters. One other word of caution before venturing down this path: It is not a perfect system. Sites that you might consider appropriate, like a student blog, might come up as filtered if you select the "Limit Adult Content" option in the website filter settings (Figure 8.3).

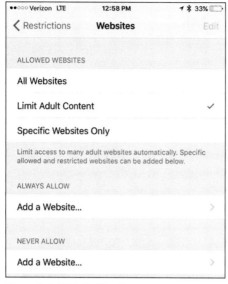

Figure 8.3 Website filter feature.

When this setting is enabled, if a child is surfing the web and comes across a blocked site, they have to enter the restriction passcode to add it to the "allowable" list of websites. At this point they would have to bring you their phone and ask you to enter the restriction passcode you chose when you set up the restrictions. Only then will they be able to access the site.

Furthermore, you could enter an even more extreme mode of web filtering by allowing only specific websites. This could be potentially time consuming, but for a child who likes to surf and get into mischief online or for one who is having a hard time concentrating on a project or assignment, it's a handy resource to have in your back pocket.

iMessage Sharing and Forwarding

As was mentioned in some of the Chapter 7 scenarios, text message exchanges can involve a lot of drama. Phone bills can tell you when texts are being received and sent, but not the content of those messages. If you want to view these as a parent, you need to have access to your child's Apple ID, and then you can see what is being sent between iPhones. (Note: If it's to another type of phone, it will only be a text message and will not be viewable via a shared account.)

By going into message settings, you can see what accounts are set up to send and receive. The Apple ID listed in there is the one you'll want to put on your device. You can have more than one email and Apple ID on your own iOS device, so this won't disrupt any messages you receive and send.

Your child will receive an email notice that this account was added to another device, which is a good opportunity to let them know that you can see anything they send or receive from their phone. You can also select which devices get forwarded any conversations taking place on the device in these settings (Figure 8.4).

You might be wondering what prevents them from going in and disabling this feature. If you have a child who seems to be especially combative on this front, you can actually disable the ability to alter accounts (in the restrictions

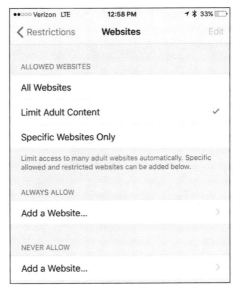

Figure 8.4 Setting up text message forwarding.

menu). This means that they will need the restrictions passcode in order to make changes to their email, text message, or social media accounts.

Why this is helpful? Any iMessage your child receives means you'll also receive and see the entire conversation. If for some reason your child deletes the conversation from their phone, you will still have a copy of it. Also, with the ability to make account changes disabled, your child won't be able to add or switch accounts (especially if you think he/she has another Apple ID).

For the full set of instructions on how to do this, visit this post: mrhook.it/imessage.

Other Options for Viewing Text Messages (Dependent on Carrier)

At this point I'll mention again that actually asking for your child's phone to look at their text messages on occasion can be the greatest deterrent to inappropriate conversations. However, if you feel, based on your child's behavior, that there is still something potentially happening via text messages or social media, there are more options for you through your cell phone provider.

For example, Sprint has the option to limit who your child can send to, and also who they receive from. Going to the sprint.com website and going into your "my preferences" section gives you the ability to set limits and permissions and check the option for text(s). This allows you to select the device you want to control and then provides a number of options to:

- Not block text messages (basically the option to unblock, if you've blocked earlier)

- Block all text, inbound and outbound

- Block all inbound text

- lock all outbound text

- BLOCK ONLY "these" numbers for inbound/outbound

- ALLOW ONLY "these" numbers for inbound/outbound text

Why is this helpful? With the last option, you could set up your child's phone so that it only receives texts from preapproved people. This is especially helpful if your child is involved in a situation of harassment or bullying. It can also be a handy option to have on hand should your or their cell phone number ever be used as spam for advertisers. You can block those messages and senders in this section of your permissions.

Although this example is Sprint specific, other major cell phone providers (T-Mobile, Verizon) offer similar plans or features that let you dictate who can send and receive calls and texts on a particular device. Contact your cell service provider for more information.

Helping Focus with Guided Access

Some restrictions help with apps or websites, but there are also times when your child may need some help with focus. Any type of mobile device comes with its share of distractions. Phones and tablets have pop-up notifications, and this has now stretched to laptops and desktops as well. On a device that allows multiple windows, you now have multiple sites and programs vying for your attention.

In the iOS world, you now have the option to "multitask" between two apps, but generally the number of programs that can distract you is limited. However, kids will still feel the need to switch between apps on occasion and could potentially get sucked into social media or binge-watching Minecraft videos on YouTube. Enter guided access and the ability to lock in apps.

Located under the general settings and buried in the next level of accessibility settings is where you can locate guided access (Figure 8.5). Turning on guided access requires yet another passcode (different from the passcode lock and the restriction lock). Once

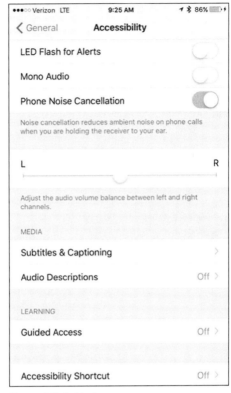

Figure 8.5 Guided access

enabled, with a triple-click of the home button, you can enable single-app mode, which force-locks the device into an app until you enter the passcode to release it.

The updated version actually lets you lock into the app for a predetermined time period as well, so you can set the lock for 30 minutes so that your child focuses on a particular website or app for that chunk of time.

A quick story here to proclaim the success of this particular restriction with a family in our community. I had shared the guided access feature during a parent night, and the very next day I received a phone call. One particular mother had been struggling with her son's ability to focus on an app (in this case an ebook that he had to study). The night after our talk, she went home to test out this feature. Her son was reading his ebook as usual, and as usual, he would switch to Facebook after about 2 minutes of reading.

When he stepped away, she took his iPad and enabled guided access mode. When her son returned to finish his work, she left his room and headed downstairs. Before her foot hit the first step she heard a loud *"Mom!"* and knew she had succeeded (as he had tried and failed to exit the app).

Internet Filtering

As was mentioned earlier, filtering the internet is only successful when devices are connected to it. With smartphones, internet access is only a mildly strong cell signal away. That said, it's advisable to have some level of filtering on your home devices as well as any school-issued ones. Enter my disclaimer here once again: A strong internet filter is no substitute for strong parenting.

OpenDNS

OpenDNS (opendns.com) is a free online filter with some upgrades available for a price. While it's geared mainly to protect against virus and phishing attacks, there are now ways you can set up parental controls. One of the great things about OpenDNS is that you can set up web filtering at the router level and differentiate based on devices. So that means that your kids' devices can have different filter settings than your own devices.

Circle Home and Go

This is Disney's entry into the fray of internet filtering. It provides a plug 'n' play device for $99 that connects to your home network. Then using an accompanying Circle Home app, you can set limits on internet connectivity and screen time for all Wi-Fi–enabled devices. Using the Circle Go app extends that filtering and oversight to mobile devices not at the home (for a cost of $9.99/month). Learn more at meetcircle.com.

Tracking and Spying Programs

In addition to filters that extend out of the home like Circle Go, there is a growing trend in services that allow you to track and monitor your kids' accounts and devices. These tracking programs walk a fine line between giving your kids some of their own space to learn and grow and spying on their every move. Key logger programs do much of the same things on computers where you can see transcripts of every keystroke made on a laptop or desktop. This could be useful to prompt a conversation, but you also run a risk as a parent of losing trust and communication with your child.

The filter market is flooded with many different options, and some now extend to mobile devices. As these change so frequently, I won't spend a lot of time going over them, but what follows are a few that I've discovered or that families have used in the past that seem to do a fair job of protecting kids from inappropriate content.

Of the multitude of tracking programs out there, TeenSafe (www.teensafe.com) seems to be the most popular, with already over a half a million users as of summer of 2016. TeenSafe allows parents to monitor kids' social media accounts, their text messages, and who they are on the phone with, and also track their location. All of this comes at a cost of $14.95 per month and the additional risk that your child may feel there is a lack of trust between you.

Other Paid Services

Net Nanny, McAfee, and K9 web protection each offer different feature sets at a yearly or monthly price. Net Nanny (netnanny.com) seems to be the favorite of communities and ratings systems, as it's specifically geared toward parental controls and filtering on children's devices. Combining the services of Net Nanny or OpenDNS with the built-in website restrictions of iOS, and you'd have a pretty powerful combination protecting your kids.

The Ultimate Safety Device: A "Dumb Phone"

When filters, restrictions, and monitoring don't seem to be helping your situation, you could go the extreme route and give your kids a "dumb phone." In talking with parents, many claim the need to be able to connect with their kids either via a phone call or text message. Since smartphones come with these features but also a host of other avenues of communication, giving your child a phone with only calling and texting features might be the answer.

However, with the continually increasing smartphone market coupled with the decrease in cost of those devices, this option may soon be gone. Which leaves only the ultimate option for keeping your kid safe: not giving them a device at all. Just know that every action has a consequence, and ultimately, it's best to work with your kids on tackling these modern digital problems head-on and as a team. By choosing to shut out the digital world, you kick the can down the road to when your child leaves your home and now has access to this forbidden world—with no knowledge base or wisdom on how to navigate it.

CHAPTER 9

TYING IT ALL TOGETHER

As with every book in this series, it's important to see where each puzzle piece fits in the mobile learning initiative. While the focus of learning is the student, parents and the community play a large role in that process, especially when devices go home and learning takes place online or on the device. A parent needs to be in communication with the teacher about which programs, apps, and websites their child will need to access. Parents need to work with the technology department on necessary forms or recommendations for how to best filter and support the device at home. Conversations with the campus and district administration about behavior and expectations need to be open and transparent. Although in some districts this is not a requirement, or is considered a luxury, some level of parent training by the instructional coaches needs to be happening, too.

District Administration

When a mobile device initiative launches, the majority of the communication tends to come from district administration. In addition to public forums, board meetings, and interaction with staff, it is a good idea for district administration to seek some level of support and feedback from the community. As these devices will spend the majority of their day in the home (for districts that allow them to go home, or in the case of BYOD), there should be some level of support in that area.

In addition to garnering support and listening to concerns, there are usually some legal forms that are required if the device is school issued. Will there be an option for insurance? What are the consequences for misuse? Where does the student data live, and who can see it? In the past decade, there has been an awareness in school districts to greatly adapt and modify their acceptable use policy (AUP) for technology. In the case of my district, we evolved our AUP into responsible use guidelines (RUG) for technology to put more onus and action on the student to be responsible. In addition, while earlier policies only threw a blanket of protection over the district network and devices, we expanded ours to include personal devices that were brought on campus.

These forms and frequently asked questions should be easily accessible for parents in a mobile device initiative. Another thing I've advised districts to do is to have a point person for any questions or feedback that come up. In some cases those questions may be technical in nature (how does my student log in to a particular website?) or behavioral (my kid is distracted by another kid's use of technology or is being cyberbullied). While the point person may not be able to handle the conflict or concern directly, they can route you to the appropriate person in the district who can. Of course, the larger the district, the harder it might be to find a point person. My district of 8,000 students is still relatively small, and I make myself available and open to parents on a regular basis. In larger districts, the principal is generally the point person for such calls and concerns.

Campus Administration

In most cases, campus administration will be the leaders of the initiative on their campus. As such, they will often organize the parent nights or PTA meetings that revolve around the mobile device initiative. When discipline issues arise with technology, as with non–technology-related discipline issues, they are also where the buck stops. However, know that they also have other duties, including being the instructional leader for their campus, helping with human resources, working on campus finances, and putting out day-to-day fires as they crop up.

I say this to give you some level of empathy for their plight, but also to make you aware that there are usually various levels of concern with technology that would make their way up to a campus principal. A difficult situation with a teacher that you have tried communicating with but isn't getting resolved, or a more general concern that involves the safety of your child, should definitely be brought to their attention. Things like your child playing a game for too long online might be something that could be brought to the attention of the instructional coaches or instruction technology department for support.

As I mentioned in Chapter 2 about things not to do, the first thing is to not take away the device when your child does something wrong online or with the device. Although in certain extreme cases, that may ultimately be the solution, for schools it's much the same rule. Many of the instructional materials and textbooks are now only available in a digital version. Although this lends itself to more flexibility (no more "the dog ate my homework" stories) and organizationally ("I lost that worksheet!"), it also means that the student needs access to the device or the internet in some capacity. Campuses may have their own set of consequences for device and behavioral infractions, but because the device is used for instructional purposes, taking it away is only temporary measure to correct an issue. In Figure 9.1, notice that whenever a child reaches the second offense involving their device, they must take a screen shot of whatever the offense was and then send an email to the parent and copy the teacher. This has been a great deterrent in our district for off-task behavior and acts as an instant form of communication between teacher and parent.

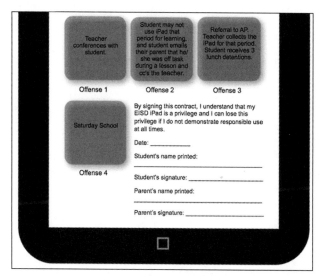

Figure 9.1 iPad Oath, by Lisa Johnson (http://mrhook.it/oath)

Classroom Teacher

As mentioned earlier for the behavior issue and expectations about mobile devices, the most frequent interactions involving student devices will be with the teacher. They will be the front line for any technical or behavioral issues, and in many cases, they will be the ones feeling the pain of any issues that arise in either of those fields.

Teachers are also the main point of contact for you as a parent. While each teacher may have different levels of expectations, or intend different uses of devices for learning, there are generally some ground rules agreed upon by all teachers at a grade level or campus. One of the most basic expectations that we encountered quite often with our secondary students was that the devices would be charged overnight every night. Although this seems like a small thing to ask, it can make a big difference in the classroom experience for your child if they are forced to sit in the corner charging their device by a plug or having to fill out a paper version of a dynamic assignment because they didn't come to school prepared.

One thing I preach to parents in my workshops or talks is to be patient with the classroom teacher. They have to manage a set of learning standards, high-stakes assessments, and behavior problems on a daily basis, and for some, the change to a mobile device initiative is another level of stress or fear that they might struggle with at first. While there is an expectation that the device come to school charged and ready, there may also be days where it is not needed.

One of the great benefits of a mobile learning initiative is the degree to which a teacher can differentiate assignments. For some, that might mean one group does a traditional paper-and-pencil task while another group works on some online research, and yet another group is collaborating online for a larger project. Some of this was possible before technology, but the flexibility and ease with which it can happen today can really accelerate deeper under-standing of learning objectives. Keep that in mind when communicating with a particularly stressed teacher, but also be open to supporting the learning at home and ask the teacher for any ideas on how you can help on that front.

Technology Department

Technology departments in some districts can range from one person to hundreds of technicians, depending on the size of district and the number of devices they are supporting. Their role in a mobile device initiative is to keep the devices operational (in the case of school-issued devices) or to make sure the network is safe and stable enough for learning to happen.

In the case of school-issued devices, that level of support may be needed almost 24/7. With learning taking place online at school and home, there are times where you may need to contact someone to help support a device that is broken or not working correctly. Some districts keep a hotline or email address for such issues. Some also keep some sort of "office hours" for check-in support. In our district, we encourage students to keep their devices over the summer, but that also means we have a time each week where students can come in for technical support.

In the case of loss or damage, the technology department is also the point person for issuing a new or temporary device, collecting money for repairs or insurance, and in some cases, helping track down a lost or stolen device. In our district we used a laser etcher to place a phone number, bar code, and logo on the back of the device. This acts not just as an easy-to-see number for parents to call, but in some cases, as a theft deterrent.

A couple of years ago, when we first allowed older students to take their devices home, I had a student approach me in tears. He told me that his device had been stolen while he was on vacation with his family. We had actually received a call from a pawn shop near Harvard that had recovered the device and saw the number on the back (the thieves had covered it with duct tape). When the pawn shop saw the logo and number, they immediately called us and then shipped it back to the district. When the student approached us, we handed him his device back. His answer? "This is great! Did you get my stolen watch, too?"

As someone who has worked in a technology department before, I can tell you that no one calls to tell them they are doing a good job or to tell them how well the Wi-Fi is working. Every call or email usually represents a problem or issue. We've been extremely fortunate to have a technology department that researches best practices and makes adjustments for issues before they happen. But even then, sometimes things slip through the cracks. Be patient, thoughtful, and thankful for their support, and know that your child's technical problem may be one of hundreds they are solving at that moment.

Instructional Coaches

The role of the instructional coach or educational technologist is to support the teachers with strategies, websites, apps, and best practices for mobile learning. In the more forward-thinking districts, they also provide support for families in the form of training and resources for parents. In the book on instructional coaching, I outlined a few different ways to go about doing this.

Some districts might not have the level of funding or support needed for these positions, so in some cases this may fall on a person in the central office or on the librarian. Regardless, there should be a person in the district (see the "point person" I mentioned in the section on district administration) who provides some level of instructional support for parents in a mobile device initiative.

Parent learning can happen during the school day, during a portion of a booster club meeting, or even during a parent-teacher conference. Many districts will provide some level of parent orientation when first introducing mobile devices to help with ideas for home and to handle questions. While this is not mandatory, you can request that this be provided in some fashion for parents in the district.

In our district, we started professional learning with parents in the most familiar format, face to face. But as the initiative continued, we added in other components. One was hosting a parent panel discussion (mrhook.it/panel) that got community members to have conversations about mobile learning and tools they can use to help with it at home. This was a great way to build capacity within the community, as groups of parents could discuss their concerns or strategies for raising a kid in the digital age.

Because many parents work during the day or night, the other way to get support is through online resources such as Common Sense Media (commonsensemedia.org), as I've mentioned in earlier chapters, or through taking an online course. Although there are a few more options out there now, I built this iTunes U course in 2014 for that very purpose: mrhook.it/101. I purposely made it available only on iOS devices, because our students had iPads and I wanted the parents to model the use of the device as a tool for learning as well.

Regardless of learning method or style, as a parent in a mobile device initiative, know that you can add to the level of success of your child in this new environment by keeping informed and by learning alongside them.

CHAPTER 10

BUILDING A POSITIVE DIGITAL LIFESTYLE

In my interview in Chapter 3 with digital child-rearing advocate Devorah Heitner, she mentioned that what we do and how we act around technology affects our own kids' point of view of it. In one of the first parent meetings I ever held in this position in 2009, I asked a diverse group of elementary parents what a digital footprint was.

The answers varied, but many came to the conclusion that basically everything a child posts online makes up their footprint. Some questioned whether "footprint" was the proper analogy, as footprints eventually fade or get washed away, but what's posted online has a certain amount of permanence. Some in the group mentioned this was more of a "digital tattoo" (a phrase I've heard other edtech leaders use) than a footprint.

What happened next was pretty mind-blowing to me as both a parent and a leader in the field. A mom stood up and said that it was the responsibility of all the parents in the room to start building their child's brand from day one. She mentioned that she made sure to purchase the domain name of each of her kids even *before* they were born. While some parents laughed this off, it definitely left an impression on many of them.

Had they already been building their children's digital profile without knowing it? Posting photos of their first lost tooth on Facebook or videos of their first successful bike ride on YouTube leaves behind a digital shadow of sorts around their kid's overall footprint.

At a recent digital citizenship event at one of our middle schools, we asked kids to Google themselves. Most of them discovered nothing, but a few students found images or posts about them that they weren't even aware of. One child found pictures of himself in a bathing suit that his parents had shared on a local newspaper website. While he was embarrassed by the photo, he was more upset with the fact that it was posted without him knowing about it. When he asked me to take it down, I told him I didn't have that kind of authority, and it was his mission now to figure out how to contact the newspaper and ask for it to be removed. He quickly discovered that it is much easier to post a picture somewhere than it is to remove it.

A Digital Portfolio

While all of these digital tools and social media sites may seem threatening, they can actually help your child later in life when they apply for college or a job. In our district, we are working with high school students to publish and showcase their best work on the web, either via a blog or with a digital portfolio tool like Bulb (bulbapp.com).

Creating these online portfolios empowers your child to turn social media and their best work into a powerful ally for their future. According to a latest CareerBuilder study, 60 percent of employers use social media to research job candidates (mrhook.it/career). Compare that number to the 11 percent that searched social media in 2006, and you can predict that it will only continue to increase in the future.

When They Leave Your House

Parenting has never been harder than in the digital age. In the past, parents could lock the windows and doors to prevent kids from leaving or strangers from entering. Now with the internet, there is no way to completely lock out and protect your child from the outside world (short of removing any internet-enabled device in your household).

And that vulnerability might not be a bad thing.

Although we want to protect our kids from the dangers and bullies online, we also want them to be prepared to deal with those problems when they get older. When I'm talking with parents, I often use the analogy of training wheels on a bicycle. If we keep the training wheels all the way through a kid's educational career, when they finally leave the home at 18 and the training wheels come off, will they be able to keep the bike upright on their own? Maybe they can ride for a little while before falling, but then when they look to you for support, you won't be there.

The same can be said with online interactions. While each child is different and may require different degrees of security and limitation when it comes to technology, having interactions and discussions about things they are encountering online helps build up their wisdom and their decision making in the future when they leave your house. They will have learned how to ride the bike, fall, and recover.

"Lemonade for Dylan"

I shared this story in my book for district administrators, too, but as it directly involves a parent and student interaction, I find it appropriate to share here as well.

In the spring of 2013 I was approached by an elementary school parent. She started a sentence with "I need to talk to you about *these iPads.* ..." Having gone through several parent meetings, phone calls, and discussions, I was fully prepared to hear a horror story about how her child had done something inappropriate on the device. The phrase "*these iPads*" made it sound as if they were some sort of bad influence from outside.

However, I was not only surprised by what happened next, it affected my life going forward. She shared with me the story of her fourth grade daughter (for the sake of this story, we'll call her "Clara"). Clara had a 2-year-old nephew named Dylan who suffered from a rare neurodegenerative disorder called Krabbe's disease. Although the disease is ultimately fatal, Clara wanted to do something to help her nephew.

So she did what any 10-year-old does trying to raise money—she started a lemonade stand. Although she was able to collect $50 or $60 that way, she felt like it wasn't enough. She asked her mom if she could build a website to help raise more money for Dylan and the larger organization Hunter's Hope (huntershope.org). Her mom told her about their uncle, who was a web developer, but before she could even finish her sentence, Clara interrupted with "No, Mom—I want to make the site myself." She went on to explain that during the school year, students in her fourth grade classroom had used their iPads and a website building tool called Weebly (weebly.com) to build their own websites. She wanted to design the site and use it to not only raise money for Dylan but also to coordinate other lemonade stands around the city (Figure 10.1).

I was floored. At the age of 10, this student not only used technology in a way to further her cause, she also was a project manager and planner for organizing lemonade stands all over the city. Although Dylan ultimately passed away in 2014, his hope and spirit are carried on by all those affected by his story and the story shared by his extremely motivated 10-year-old aunt.

Powerful. (lemonadefordylan.weebly.com)

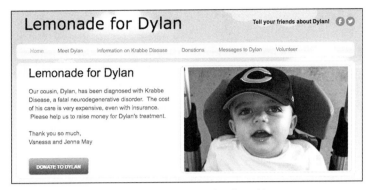

Figure 10.1 Lemonade for Dylan, a website developed by a 10-year old student to help her nephew.

Taking Time to Reflect (without Technology)

Lately I've noticed a strange phenomenon that occurs at traffic lights around town. The light turns green and the first car, after some hesitation, pulls forward. Then the next one, after another prolonged delay, does the same. This continues until maybe four or five cars have traveled through what would normally be a 10- or 12-car light. When I look over at the drivers, they are all doing the same thing: checking their phones.

I've seen a lot of commentary on the web recently about our addiction to our phones. In Chapter 4, I described the digital yawn, an event that seems to happen more and more in social settings. There are now restaurants in Beirut that actually give you a 10% discount if you turn in your phone and socialize at their restaurant. The flip side of that is that there are restaurants that give you 10% off if you catch a Pokémon GO character in their restaurant.

The use of cell phones as an extension of both our arm and our brain has caused a somewhat predictable outcry against the use of mobile devices and phones in the classroom. Too much screen time or too much time being connected are valid concerns of those who oppose the use of devices.

NPR has released a couple of thought-provoking stories in recent years, including this article titled "We Are Just Not Here Anymore" (mrhook.it/npr). In the article, the author Linton Weeks takes us through the concept of the "severed self" and asks the question, "How can we ever feel comfortable with others when we don't even feel comfortable with ourselves?" He mentions a course at the University of Washington on "Contemplative Practices" where professor David Levy actually teaches his students patience, reflection, and meditation by "unplugging" for a few minutes before class.

In September 2013, NPR's All Tech Considered released a short film titled "Forgot My Phone" by videographer Charlene deGuzman (mrhook.it/phone). It was meant to be somewhat tongue-in-cheek, but actually highlighted the fact that we aren't really present unless we are connecting and documenting our lives on our devices. I found myself both laughing and crying during the two minutes of this video.

Last, comedian Louis C.K. went on a comedic rant about cell phones on the Conan show (mrhook.it/conan). In his interview he mentions the fact that we can't truly ever be alone and "be ourselves and just sit there. Being a person." He goes on to say that "underneath everything, there's that thing … you know … that empty. That knowledge that we are all alone. It's down there." While he's a comedian, I think he's waxing poetic about the fact that we can't let ourselves ever be truly happy or truly sad because we are constantly connected.

As parents we need to work with kids (and ourselves) in balancing our lives in every way. We talk with them about eating right, about manners, about how to behave in various situations. I'm going to argue it's time we talk to them about when it's OK not to connect. When it's OK to just "be."

I've struggled with this personally, as I've always felt my phone was an extension of my hand. Then, several months ago, one of my daughters told me, "Daddy, can you put down your phone and pay attention to me?" It broke my heart, but also alerted me to a larger problem. The message I was sending her then 4-year-old mind was that the phone was more important to me than she was. I also found myself feeding our youngest daughter her bottle at night with one hand while I was checking Twitter on my phone with in the other. I was missing that magical moment of physical connection with her, because of my need to have a virtual one with people all over the world.

So I decided to change.

I started to enforce these five simple rules for myself:

1. When I get home, the phone gets plugged into the charger, and that's where it sits the whole night.

2. While the kids are awake, I don't work, connect, tweet, blog, or anything. I just spend time with my family.

3. When feeding the baby and getting her to go to sleep, no technology whatsoever.

4. After the kids are in bed, unless it's a major project, I don't work or tweet or blog. I spend time with my wife watching a show, washing dishes, or cleaning up toys—or just talking.

5. The phone stays downstairs, connected to the charger, all night. It doesn't go into my bedroom.

Though I haven't followed these rules every single day, I find them easy enough to maintain and actually find that I'm working a lot more efficiently because of my disconnection. When feeding our youngest her bottle at night, I take the time to connect with her, but I also use that time as sort of "reflection meditation" if you will. I reflect and evaluate my day. I think about creative projects that I need to start or problems that I need to solve.

I discovered that I can just "be alone" digitally and the world will move along regardless. By doing this I was also modeling for my kids how and when to interact with technology.

For our kids it's much the same experience, if not even more extreme. While we moved into this constantly connected world late in life, they were born into it. The challenge of just being quiet and still without connecting can be a challenge.

Some recent research out of the United Kingdom suggest that being bored can actually help kids with creative ideas, stress, and goal setting (mrhook. it/bored). In the research, they discovered that people who were essentially forced to be bored rather than being distracted by their devices actually had more creative ideas about mundane tasks. Students in the University of Washington course I mentioned earlier found the practice of unplugging before class tedious and boring at the beginning of the semester. But after a time, they found that time to be not only peaceful and reflective, but also helpful to their mindfulness, creativity, and productivity going forward.

So the next time you are at that traffic light or in that waiting room, hold off on taking out your phone and checking it, even if it hurts. Instead, take a moment to breathe in life.

Reflect.

Think.

And just "be."

Your kids will thank you for it.

REFERENCES

Common Sense Media. (2015). *Common sense census: Media use by tweens and teens* [infographic]. Retrieved from https://www.commonsensemedia.org/the-common-sense-census-media-use-by-tweens-and-teens-infographic

Higgins, S; Xiao, Z., & Katsipataki, M. (2012). *The impact of digital technology on learning: A summary for the Education Endowment Foundation.* Retrieved from https://v1.educationendowmentfoundation.org.uk/uploads/pdf/The_Impact_of_Digital_Technologies_on_Learning_(2012).pdf

Shapiro, J. (2015). *The American Academy of Pediatrics just changed their guidelines on kids and screen time.* Retrieved from http://www.forbes.com/sites/jordanshapiro/2015/09/30/the-american-academy-of-pediatrics-just-changed-their-guidelines-on-kids-and-screen-time/#67b04e57137c

Wilson, D. (2014). *Move your brain, grow your body.* Retreived from https://www.edutopia.org/blog/move-body-grow-brain-donna-wilson

ISTE STANDARDS

2016 ISTE Standards for Students

The 2016 ISTE Standards for Students emphasize the skills and qualities we want for students, enabling them to engage and thrive in a connected, digital world. The standards are designed for use by educators across the curriculum, with every age student, with a goal of cultivating these skills throughout a student's academic career. Both students and teachers will be responsible for achieving foundational technology skills to fully apply the standards. The reward, however, will be educators who skillfully mentor and inspire students to amplify learning with technology and challenge them to be agents of their own learning.

1. **Empowered Learner**

   Students leverage technology to take an active role in choosing, achieving and demonstrating competency in their learning goals, informed by the learning sciences. Students:

   a. articulate and set personal learning goals, develop strategies leveraging technology to achieve them and reflect on the learning process itself to improve learning outcomes.

   b. build networks and customize their learning environments in ways that support the learning process.

   c. use technology to seek feedback that informs and improves their practice and to demonstrate their learning in a variety of ways.

   d. understand the fundamental concepts of technology operations, demonstrate the ability to choose, use and troubleshoot current technologies and are able to transfer their knowledge to explore emerging technologies.

2. Digital Citizen

Students recognize the rights, responsibilities and opportunities of living, learning and working in an interconnected digital world, and they act and model in ways that are safe, legal and ethical. Students:

a. cultivate and manage their digital identity and reputation and are aware of the permanence of their actions in the digital world.

b. engage in positive, safe, legal and ethical behavior when using technology, including social interactions online or when using networked devices.

c. demonstrate an understanding of and respect for the rights and obligations of using and sharing intellectual property.

d. manage their personal data to maintain digital privacy and security and are aware of data-collection technology used to track their navigation online.

3. Knowledge Constructor

Students critically curate a variety of resources using digital tools to construct knowledge, produce creative artifacts and make meaningful learning experiences for themselves and others. Students:

a. plan and employ effective research strategies to locate information and other resources for their intellectual or creative pursuits.

b. evaluate the accuracy, perspective, credibility and relevance of information, media, data or other resources.

c. curate information from digital resources using a variety of tools and methods to create collections of artifacts that demonstrate meaningful connections or conclusions.

d. build knowledge by actively exploring real-world issues and problems, developing ideas and theories and pursuing answers and solutions.

4. Innovative Designer

Students use a variety of technologies within a design process to identify and solve problems by creating new, useful or imaginative solutions. Students:

a. know and use a deliberate design process for generating ideas, testing theories, creating innovative artifacts or solving authentic problems.

b. select and use digital tools to plan and manage a design process that considers design constraints and calculated risks.

c. develop, test and refine prototypes as part of a cyclical design process.

d. exhibit a tolerance for ambiguity, perseverance and the capacity to work with open-ended problems.

5. Computational Thinker

Students develop and employ strategies for understanding and solving problems in ways that leverage the power of technological methods to develop and test solutions. Students:

a. formulate problem definitions suited for technology-assisted methods such as data analysis, abstract models and algorithmic thinking in exploring and finding solutions.

b. collect data or identify relevant data sets, use digital tools to analyze them, and represent data in various ways to facilitate problem-solving and decision-making.

c. break problems into component parts, extract key information, and develop descriptive models to understand complex systems or facilitate problem-solving.

d. understand how automation works and use algorithmic thinking to develop a sequence of steps to create and test automated solutions.

6. Creative Communicator

Students communicate clearly and express themselves creatively for a variety of purposes using the platforms, tools, styles, formats and digital media appropriate to their goals. Students:

a. choose the appropriate platforms and tools for meeting the desired objectives of their creation or communication.

b. create original works or responsibly repurpose or remix digital resources into new creations.

c. communicate complex ideas clearly and effectively by creating or using a variety of digital objects such as visualizations, models or simulations.

d. publish or present content that customizes the message and medium for their intended audiences.

7. Global Collaborator

Students use digital tools to broaden their perspectives and enrich their learning by collaborating with others and working effectively in teams locally and globally. Students:

a. use digital tools to connect with learners from a variety of backgrounds and cultures, engaging with them in ways that broaden mutual understanding and learning.

b. use collaborative technologies to work with others, including peers, experts or community members, to examine issues and problems from multiple viewpoints.

c. contribute constructively to project teams, assuming various roles and responsibilities to work effectively toward a common goal.

d. explore local and global issues and use collaborative technologies to work with others to investigate solutions.

ISTE Standards·S © 2016 International Society for Technology in Education. ISTE® is a registered trademark of the International Society for Technology in Education. If you would like to reproduce this material, please contact permissions@iste.org.